THE MANAGEMENT OF INTERNATIONAL BANKS

The second edition of this book has been written in the context of the wave of international loan reschedulings in 1982 which has not only called in question the assumptions underlying many banks' international strategies but also evoked the possibility of a seizing up and collapse of the international banking structure.

The book analyses how the management of national banks with an international function have developed their strategy, selected their product/market/client mix, organised their human resources, developed operating systems and overseas networks and dealt with issues of treasury and asset management.

Throughout the book, emphasis is placed on how managers have dealt with such critical issues as the deterioration of the risk/reward ratio in international lending, the effective mobilisation of necessary human resources, the challenge of competition, and the imperative of profit maximisation. The evolution of challenge and response along a typical international 'life cycle' is described. Surveys of bankers' behaviour by the author and others supplement analysis of statistical data to produce a profile of management behaviour of interest to newcomers to banking, clients, regulators, analysts and other constituencies of the international banking sector.

Steven I. Davis is the Chief Executive of DIBC (UK) Ltd, an international banking consulting firm based in London. He is the author of *The Euro-Bank*.

INTERNATIONAL BANKING SERIES

General editor: Steven I. Davis

Steven I. Davis:	*The Management of International Banks*
T. H. Donaldson:	*Lending in International Commercial Banking*
Nigel R. L. Hudson:	*Money and Exchange Dealing in International Banking*

THE MANAGEMENT OF INTERNATIONAL BANKS

Steven I. Davis

First edition (The Management Function
in International Banking) *1979*
Reprinted 1983
Second edition (The Management of International
Banks) *1983*

Published by
MACMILLAN PUBLISHERS LTD
(*Journals Division*)
and distributed by
Globe Book Services Ltd
Canada Road, Byfleet
Surrey KT14 7JL, England

ISBN 0 333 35034 0

Filmsetting by Vantage Photosetting Co Ltd
Eastleigh and London

Printed in Hong Kong

To my friends, colleagues and
family who supported:
Constantia et Pertinacia

Contents

List of Tables and Figures

FIGURES

Editor's and Author's Preface

In the summer of 1975, amidst the alarums and excursions of the aftermath of the 1974 international banking crisis of confidence, I made a first effort to fill a perceived gap in books written about international banking by practising – and I hope knowledgeable – bankers. What emerged was *The Euro-Bank: Its Origins, Management and Outlook* – a volume dealing with purely international, or Euro-banks, operating in the London market.

Three years later, my brief was more ambitious – but, at the same time, more modest from a personal standpoint. The overseas activities of national banks throughout the world dwarf those of the Euro-banks and raise a variety of issues relating to the allocation of resources between domestic and international business. To deal with the immense breadth and specialised nature of these activities, I suggested, and Macmillan agreed, that the appropriate solution was to ask experienced professionals in individual aspects of international banking such as lending and money dealing to write individual volumes on their sectors of interest which, taken together, would constitute a series of books providing a reasonably complete guide to actual international banking practice for the student, newcomer, or outside observer of the international banking scene.

In the four years which have passed since the first edition of this book was written, the trends visible then have been accentuated: even more intense competition with a depressing impact on gross margins, greater sophistication of corporate clients, the need to differentiate one's bank from an increasingly homogeneous pack of competitors and the growing importance of sovereign risk exposure. International banking has come a long way from its relatively passive, 'foreign department' status of the 1960s and earlier; it is truly big business for the major national banks in the world who have been obliged to move abroad to sustain earnings growth and protect their domestic clientele from the ravages of foreign competition. The senior international banker has been obliged by these external and internal challenges to become in many aspects more of a manager than a banker, a revolutionary development in a traditional industry where promotion has usually been a function of success in the business of lending money.

With the above-mentioned specialist banking sectors well covered by Messrs Donaldson and Hudson, I have, therefore, appropriated for myself the topic of the management function in international banking – one which is now the focus of my own consulting practice following 20 years as an international banker. My approach has been to provide in this volume an overall framework or 'umbrella' for the other books in the series, in which such central issues as the determination of objectives and organisational structures are analysed. While there is inevitably a bit of overlap – or even conflict! – with the other volumes, my intention has been to write this book from the perspective of the individual or individuals with overall responsibility for the international function. The book is what my good friend Professor Charles Williams of the Harvard Business School would call 'issue-oriented'; it tries to explain management behaviour within a framework of what can be regarded as the principal issues facing international bank managers. As a practising member of this fraternity, I have tried to maintain that delicate balance between understanding and objectivity. Whether successful or not in this endeavour, I hope that the book is useful to those for whom it is written: students of banking, newcomers to the trade of international banking, and outside observers such as central bankers, customers and academics who are trying to fit our behaviour into their own frame of reference.

In preparing the second edition of this book in late 1982, I have attempted to incorporate a variety of trends and perspectives brought out by the passage of four years. First, my perspective as a management consultant to banks rather than an actor on the banking stage provides a totally new and broader understanding of management behaviour. Second, many of the trends visible in 1978 have evolved to the point where they are forcing some very unpleasant choices on management. Finally, whereas international banking in the mid-1970s could be said to be a dynamic, expansive sector, in the early 1980s it is decidedly mature with even a few grey hairs showing.

My grateful thanks for their goodwill and material assistance in the preparation of this book go first to the 40 senior bankers who took the time for the first edition to fill out and discuss a detailed questionnaire on how they run their international functions, as well as the 30 senior corporate officers who provided their frank views on the performance of international banks. I can only hope that they derive from this dialogue as recorded in the book a fraction of the usefulness it has been to me in broadening my own perspective as well as quantifying management and client behaviour and attitudes. In writing the second edition of this book, my research labours were considerably assisted by those who have made a special effort to produce data on international banks: Tom Hanley of Salomon Brothers, John Rudy of Greenwich Research Associates, Brooks Chamberlin of Towers, Perrin, Forster and Crosby, Robin Monroe-Davies of IBCA (International Bank Credit Analysis), and the staff of the OECD, the Institute of Bankers Library, the Bank For International Settlements and the US Comptroller of the Currency. A special note of thanks goes to Dolores Mulroy, who somehow found the time from her work at DIBC to prepare the typescript for the second edition.

Steven I. Davis
London

1 Introduction

This book is one of a series of volumes on the actual practice of international banking written by senior bankers with considerable experience in the specific sector which is the subject of their particular book. While market practitioners may not be the most articulate spokesmen of their trade, it is to be hoped that they bring to bear a unique insight which may not be provided by an outside expert.

Within this framework, *The Management of International Banks* has two specific objectives. First, it is intended to provide the contextual framework for the series by briefly describing today's international banking market and its antecedent institutions. Its second and more important objective is to examine the role played by the senior management of an international banking department or function and to determine how such issues as the setting of overall strategy, establishing an organisation structure and the management of an overseas network are resolved by different institutions. Other volumes in the Macmillan series will focus more specifically on such critical operational sectors as the lending function and money dealing and liability management. The viewpoint of this particular book will tend to be that of the head of the international department or possibly the chief executive of the bank, while the reference points of the other volumes will be those of his subordinates responsible for or actively carrying out the specific functions described.

It might be useful at the outset to define the parameters of our subject and explain some of the methodology used in this volume. By 'international banking' is meant the activities of a bank outside its traditional domestic market sphere which involve, to a significant extent, a risk, structure or transaction not encountered domestically – whether it be the traditional 'sovereign' risk such as foreign exchange availability and arbitrary acts of a foreign government, a network set up specifically for overseas business, or a foreign exchange dealing function. Whereas in the 1970s such a distinction was sufficiently clear to provide the basis for organisational and other structures, by the early 1980s it was becoming harder to define international banking because of the global nature of client needs, the breakdown of regulatory and other artificial barriers and the growth of truly global institutions who have long outgrown their domestic market.

Our focus is, therefore, on the activities of domestic or national banks which have a non-domestic character. A separate volume, *The Euro-Bank: its Origins, Management and Outlook*, deals specifically with international banks, established and separately capitalised primarily to carry on an international Euro-currency market activity without the domestic market base of the banks discussed in this book.[1]

A second distinguishing feature is a concentration on banks whose principal activity is commercial banking – essentially the earning of interest differential income from the positive spread between loans and deposits. While this definition certainly embraces the so-called universal banks in Europe and elsewhere which have a significant capital market activity as well, it does not include institutions such as the US investment banks which are primarily engaged in the arrangement of finance and capital market operations.

In keeping with the behavioural, pragmatic approach of the series, the methodology used is an examination of actual management practices. Statistics will be used where appropriate to illustrate this practice rather than simply to describe market structures or current operating conditions. A substantial effort has been made to reflect international management practice of banks throughout the world. Several useful books have incorporated the views on key management topics of American bankers,[2] who not only represent the largest single segment of the international market, but also tend to be more forthcoming with views and statistics then their European or Asian counterparts.

INTERNATIONAL BANK AND CUSTOMER QUESTIONNAIRES

To provide such a broader and more balanced approach – as well as to compensate for the author's background and consequent limitations as a US banker! – the heads of international departments or their key associates in 40 national banks based in the US, Europe and Asia were interviewed in depth using a detailed questionnaire for the first edition in 1978. In some instances it has been possible in the text to quantify statistically the results of these interviews, but in most cases they have simply served to substantiate in a more general form the points made in individual chapters. The sample includes eighteen US, three Canadian, two British, thirteen continental European and four Asian banks; these institutions are listed in Appendix A. A conscious effort was made to obtain a reasonably representative cross section of banks based on such factors as the relative importance of a given country in the Euro-markets – hence the high proportion of US banks – and regional as opposed to money centre institutions. While some banks with a relatively small international function were included, a deliberate effort was made to weight the sample in favour of the relatively experienced and internationally sophisticated banks who have confronted today's critical issues and can discuss their proposed solutions. The questionnaire itself is attached as Appendix B.

This sample of international banks and bankers does not purport – particularly in view of the reluctance of many senior bankers to discuss management issues with outsiders – to be a professional survey using appropriate sampling and other statistical techniques. It does, however, represent a serious effort to analyse management behaviour in a sector not particularly susceptible to easy quantification.

The survey was not repeated in this second edition for a variety of reasons. More recent samplings by the author[3] and others[4] have both provided new material and also demonstrated the shortcomings of any survey of the attitudes, policies and techniques of banks in a very wide spectrum of stages of international development. More importantly, the author's experience as a management consultant to a wide variety of banks since 1979 provides an insight into actual management behaviour which is arguably more useful to the reader.

As part of the research for Chapter 7, a questionnaire was circulated in 1978 to a large number of senior financial officers of multinational corporations and other major customers of the international banks in an effort to obtain an objective and at least partially quantifiable appraisal of the marketing efforts of these institutions. The 30 responses tabulated represent, in the author's view, a useful outside opinion on the strengths and weaknesses of such efforts – particularly in view of the relative lack of professional surveys on the subject which have been made public. Responses were received from a variety of large and medium-sized corporations located in the US, UK, Japan, Australia, Scandinavia and continental Europe; the question-naire itself is attached as Appendix C. Once again this is not designed as a scientifically determined sample, although some useful quantifiable results were obtained. Its principal purpose, however, was to bring out frank appraisals of bank performance in the solicitation and servicing of prime customers.

These two surveys are intended to fill – albeit in a very minor fashion – a portion of the statistical lacunae which today charac-terise the international banking market. While global statistics on the vital subject of sovereign risk exposure on the part of international banks have been published by the Bank for Inter-national Settlements since 1974, very few countries make avail-able the extent and nature of their own banks' international loan exposure. While individual banks are understandably modest about publicising some of their less successful loans, there is less justification for the fact that only a handful of international banks – primarily the American and Canadian institutions – provide the outside analyst with the key statistics necessary for an evaluation of the level of volume, risk and profitability of their international function. Within these constraints, however, every effort has been made to include in the text the relevant industry and individual banking statistics which have been made publicly available.

To place today's international bank manager in an appro-priate historical context, Chapter 2 provides a brief synopsis of four types of predecessor institutions: the Renaissance family-owned international merchant bankers; the commercial branch banks which financed the international trade and development of the European colonies in the nineteenth century; the invest-ment or development banks which channelled European capital exports to developing countries during the same period, and the American overseas networks established after the First World War. This chapter utilises some of the admittedly fragmentary historical evidence of management behaviour to draw some tentative conclusions which might be relevant for today's inter-national bankers.

Chapter 3 then sets the stage for the subsequent analytical chapters by characterising the Euro-currency market of the early 1980s which provides the current environment for international bank management. Without unnecessarily duplicating some of the excellent detailed volumes on the nature and structure of the market,[5] this chapter describes the challenges for today's international bank managers posed by the variety of changes in customer requirements, credit exposure, organisational complexity and other factors. Chapter 4 introduces a series of chapters on specific management subjects by a general discussion of the determination of objectives and strategy formulation, as well as the various strategic phases through which a typical bank may evolve as it moves from a passive service or 'foreign' department to a complex and aggressive 'global' function. Included in this chapter are a discussion of the motives for developing an international activity, the key elements of possible strategies which can be adopted and the actual practice of bankers in terms of the priorities they establish and the extent to which objectives and strategies are articulated.

The following chapter focuses on the products and services marketed by international banks. Emphasis is placed on how a bank's product range evolves as well as how banks attempt to develop higher value-added and more differentiated products. Chapter 6's subject matter is the geographic markets served by banks. It analyses how banks select and penetrate individual markets with a particular focus on the evolution of sovereign or country lending, which is a core activity of today's international banking sector.

Chapter 7 describes the various types of clients served by international banks and the strategy behind the market segmentation process. Given the importance of multinational corporations in the typical bank's strategy, the responses of 30 such borrowers to the questionnaire described earlier are analysed. A variety of criticisms of bank performance are expressed together with the banks' efforts to deal with these problems.

Overseas networks – the banks' delivery systems – are discussed in the next chapter, which analyses how networks evolve and the steps being taken to make them more cost-effective. The key variables and criteria to be considered in opening up overseas are evaluated.

Chapter 9 focuses on the treasury function and the factors which have motivated international banks to take a comprehensive view of all assets and liabilities to improve net interest margins while maintaining adequate liquidity. Chapter 10 deals with risk assets and the policies adopted by banks to minimise risk and maximise the reward from a given loan portfolio. Separate volumes in this series cover the lending and money-dealing functions in more detail, whereas these two chapters treat these issues from the standpoint of the bank's top management.

Organisational structure is the subject of the next chapter, which evaluates the organisational implications of the strategies discussed earlier as well as the structures developed to deal with an increasingly complex and sophisticated market. The delegation of credit authorities, relationships with the domestic arm of the bank, and the decision-making process in general are

Chapter 12 deals with the human and systems resources used to implement a given strategy: management development, evaluation and compensation, management information, operating systems and risk control. The actual performance record in international banking is discussed in the next chapter, which covers the different profitability criteria used by bankers to evaluate performance. It also summarises the limited data on international profit and loss performance made available by individual banks and gleaned from in-depth interviews.

In conclusion, Chapter 13 summarises the principal problem areas likely to be faced over the next few years by international bankers. Possible management responses to these issues and other trends which might characterise the international banking market are also covered. Particular focus is placed on the changing nature of the risk/reward relationship and possible problems stemming from sovereign risk exposure.

2 Some Patterns from International Banking History

For the international bank executive embroiled in an agonising decision in the early 1980s, the experience of bankers several hundred years ago may appear a quaint irrelevance. But even a superficial glance backwards into the literature of banking history, despite its limitations for the banking analyst, can give the thoughtful modern banker some useful perspective on his own problems.

At the risk of over-simplification and reading too much into historical accounts rarely prepared by practising bankers, one can distinguish several interesting phases of banking history which have some relevance for today's senior manager. While the magnitude and sophistication of the current international banking market force one to qualify heavily any historical parallels, it is difficult to conceive of any of today's management issues, structures or concepts which have not been confronted in one form or another over the last few hundred years of international banking practice. International banking institutions over the past five hundred years or so have been engaged either in the direct financing of international trade – essentially commercial banking – or the arrangement of loans to be placed with bank or non-bank investors – what is regarded today as investment or merchant banking. Some institutions have carried on both activities, while the original merchant bankers of the Renaissance era took speculative positions in individual commodities as well as arranged for their finance. In the following analysis of the available limited and fragmentary historical records, emphasis will be placed on the management issues faced by certain categories of institutions and how successfully individual managements dealt with these problems. With few exceptions, such as de Roover's excellent study of the Medici,[1] the banking

historian has been more concerned with the elements of historical narratives – key personalities, significant dates, the impact of
external events – as opposed to banking practice itself. As a
result there is a relative absence of the microeconomic detail
necessary to evaluate the risk and reward of the business
actually carried on and the background to management decisions taken. By piecing together a variety of such narratives,
however, it is possible to make some informed guesses as to the
issues confronted by past international bankers and how they
were resolved.

THE EARLY MERCHANT BANKING INSTITUTIONS

Four specific phases or patterns of international banking history
have been selected for this analysis on the basis of the relative
availability of information and their relevance to the modern
banking environment. The first is the international merchant
banking institution which flourished between the thirteenth and
sixteenth centuries and is characterised by such family-owned
and managed firms as the Riccardi of Lucca, the Medici and the
Fugger. In addition to commercial activity involving the pur-
chase and sale of commodities, these banks financed international trade among European countries and acted as bankers to
the sovereigns of the day.

In the absence of a generally accepted international medium
of exchange, foreign trade finance generally involved the lender
assuming not only a credit but an exchange risk as well. Extending a loan to, say, an English exporter of wool payable in Venice
in ducats at an agreed exchange rate, required lending the
English sterling at an exchange rate with the ducat which was
deemed sufficient to provide an adequate return both for the use
of the funds and the assumption of the exchange risk. Ideally,
this exchange exposure would be covered by a matching transaction – say the sale of the sterling bill to a Florentine importer –
or lending ducats repayable in sterling to the same importer, but
if the flow of trade between the countries was uneven it might
have been impossible to arrange such cover. Needless to say, if
the bill proved uncollectable, or the correspondent bank making
the collection failed, the bank lost its principal.

Lending to sovereign individuals such as the English and

Spanish monarchs, the Popes, and various members of the European nobility involved a different level of risk. These loans were generally secured by physical assets such as jewels or a stream of future revenues such as customs duties, and were applied to a variety of budgetary purposes – usually to support a military effort. A hard pressed monarch would not only pledge current revenues but also hypothetical earnings stretching years into the future. The bankers often found it necessary to refinance themselves or lend new funds to maintain their status with a royal borrower and retain some hope of recovering on earlier loans. Given the voracious financial needs of princes such as Edward I of England and the Habsburg Emperor Charles V in comparison with the capital resources of their bankers, the latter soon found themselves lending a disproportionate percentage of their total portfolio as well as a multiple of their net worth to individual sovereign entities.

These family-controlled institutions with unlimited liability of the partners usually set up a network of branches in cities close to their borrowing and deposit clientele which reported to 'home office' – Lucca in the case of the Riccardi and Florence for the Medici Bank. Headquarters laid down lending and other guidelines, but the number of weeks required in this period to transmit such a message usually obliged the branch manager to take his own counsel when a rapid decision had to be made. The Medici Bank of Florence, for example, which was the largest banking house in the fifteenth century, insisted that headquarters hire all staff to ensure a high quality of personnel; letters of credit in favour of the clergy and nobility could only be issued on a cash collateralised basis, and credit limits *vis-à-vis* other banks and certain members of the Papal Curia were recommended to the various branches.[2] Successful managers were promoted to larger branches or home office, and each manager regularly visited Florence to review his branch's progress.

The final collapse of the Medici Bank came in 1494 after several decades of decline during which individual branches were liquidated as a result of credit losses, the confiscations and physical losses stemming from civil strife, and poor management. Losses exceeding branch capital were suffered from loans to such sovereigns as the Pope, the Duke of Milan, Charles of Burgundy and Edward IV of England, who renounced their obligations or were unable to meet them.

The Riccardi, a group of Italian families who operated a more centralised banking partnership than the Medici, were the principal bankers to Edward I of England in the latter portion of the thirteenth century. Funds generated in Italy were re-lent to Edward as part of such a close relationship that the Riccardi became in effect a branch of the English government.[3] A twenty-year relationship was broken by Edward in 1294 when, apparently due to losses elsewhere, the Riccardi were unable or unwilling to meet the King's financing requirements for a forthcoming war, and the family's assets in England were confiscated.

The Fugger Bank's principal activity during its period of prominence in the sixteenth century was the financing of the Habsburg Emperors Maximilian and Charles V.[4] Funding themselves in large part on a three to six month rollover basis in the Antwerp money market, they lent at a gross margin of roughly 4 per cent per annum to the Habsburgs on a collateralised basis: the pledge of jewellery and the revenues from mines, customs and crown lands. But recovery proved difficult in the 1550s as the Habsburgs became more deeply involved in the expensive business of defending their Empire, and when the Dutch government, which had guaranteed the Emperor's obligations, defaulted in 1557, the Fuggers fired the agent who had made the original loans. Over the following century, new loans and refinancings were succeeded by formal bankruptcies by the Spanish state with work-out solutions involving reduced interest and extended maturities which affected the bulk of the Fugger's loan portfolio until 1650, when the bank was finally obliged to write off Habsburg obligations representing most of the bank's profits over the previous century.

From these tales of Renaissance merchant banking woe, the historians themselves have drawn their own conclusions. Referring to the downfall of Edward I's bankers, Richard Kaeuper points out that 'however seductive the profits and privileges awaiting the king's bankers, the relationship was inevitably fatal for them. In England the Frescobaldi, the Bardi and the Peruzzi learned this hard lesson in the course of the fourteenth century.'[5] Examining the manifold causes of the Medici collapse, de Roover focuses on the management factor: 'techniques have changed, but human problems have remained the same. How to pick out the right person and put him in the right place was as much a problem for the Medici as it is in business today.'[6] Mixing banking with politics also played a role: he refers to the 'congenital defect of ... the financial type of sedentary merchant to drift from private banking into government finance'.[7]

THE NINETEENTH-CENTURY COMMERCIAL BANKS

A second relevant stage in international banking took place during the nineteenth century when new expatriate-owned commercial banks with growing branch networks were established in developing colonial territories, principally in the British Empire, to finance the international commodity trade which was the basis of their host country's economic potential. The histories of institutions such as the Hong Kong and Shanghai Banking Corporation, the Standard Bank (now Standard and Chartered Bank) in Africa, Bank of London and South America (now part of the Lloyds Bank group) and National Bank of India (now part of Grindlays Bank Ltd), trace pioneering banking efforts in which foreign-owned and managed banks were able to survive and prosper in relatively primitive economies despite wild swings in commodity export prices, civil and military strife, sharp currency fluctuations and significant loan losses attributable to poor management judgement. In their fluid environment, some of these institutions, in the absence of an indigenous lender of last resort, often assumed such central banking attributes as that of note issue.

In most cases these institutions were managed in the field by relatively young expatriate bankers who, given a communications time lag even greater than was the case with the Medici bankers in Europe, sank or swam on their own merits. Home office – generally in London – laid down general policy guidelines: for example, BOLSA branch managers were to assume no exchange exposure in their lending book; to finance only short-term, self-liquidating trade transactions; and never to lend to local governments or against mortgages and securities.[8] Such conservative lending principles, coupled with a high level of liquidity in the face of the perennial local bank crashes, civil strife and periodic government defaults, ensured that BOLSA was one of a limited number of survivors of the nineteenth-century Latin American banking scene.

Another survivor in a different marketplace was the Hong

Kong and Shanghai Banking Corporation, which was founded in 1865 as the first bank owned by Hong Kong businessmen and dedicated to the China Trade: the three-cornered exchange of opium, tea and silk using silver as the general medium of exchange. The new bank got off to a difficult start: the Overend Gurney collapse in London brought about the failure of six of the eleven foreign-owned banks functioning in Hong Kong within a year of the Hong Kong Bank's start-up.[9] Its first two Chief Managers were asked by the Board to leave as the result of significant early loan losses.

Despite assuming both a credit and exchange risk on its loans – silver was the principal lending currency, repayable in sterling at a fixed rate – the Hong Kong Bank successfully managed both its exchange and credit exposure despite a sharp decline in the value of silver against sterling in the 1870s. Profitable branches were opened throughout the Pacific Basin as the bank followed the China Trade pattern based on China's key imports and exports. The bank became involved in sovereign risk lending on a secured basis when the Manchu Dynasty began in 1863 to borrow against the security of customs receipts which by agreement were controlled by British government officials. A number of such loans were managed by the Hong Kong Bank and sold in London and Hong Kong; its success is perhaps best described by the comment of the British head of Chinese Customs on one particular loan: 'the Bank made hugely by it'.[10] While the Manchus collapsed and the new Republican government foundered in the period prior to the First World War, the Bank continued to float successfully a variety of loans for railways and projects secured by the individual projects or specific revenue from customs or the salt monopoly.

The National Bank of India, which was engaged since its founding in 1863 in the financing of India's export and import trade, was also one of the few survivors of the crash of the 1860s associated with the Overend Gurney collapse and the opening up of the US cotton market. Branches were established in a variety of countries trading with India, despite early loan losses which resulted in the offending manager making personal restitution and another branch manager being obliged to put up a personal guaranty before assuming his new position.[11] Once again, credit as well as currency risks were taken as the bank's capital was denominated in sterling while its loans were primarily in rupees.

A final example of the nineteenth-century 'colonial' commercial bank is the Standard Bank which was set up in 1863 to finance the South African wool trade. Bad debts inevitably increased during the periodic collapses of wool prices, but exchange losses were minimised by a policy of matching currency exposures and reducing loans in Africa, rather than increasing the bank's sterling overdraft facility at home office in London.[12] Following the discovery of mineral wealth in South Africa, the bank emphasised loans against the minerals themselves rather than mortgages or equity shares; some losses, however, were still incurred when the latter declined.

THE NINETEENTH-CENTURY INVESTMENT AND UNIVERSAL BANKS

A third historical banking phenomenon was the several hundred universal banks established during the nineteenth century, one of whose principal activities was the channelling of European capital exports in the form of fixed rate, long-term loans to the developing countries of that period. In their role as promoters of railway and other projects they played the role of today's development or investment banks. Income took the form of underwriting and other fees earned on loan placements as well as interest income derived from the portion of these issues held in portfolio.

One sub-category of these universal banks was the large number of relatively new commercial banks such as the Mitsui Bank,[13] Deutsche Bank,[14] and Société Générale de Belgique,[15] established in the countries with more recent colonial interests, which also financed trade between the home country and its economic outposts abroad through a growing network of overseas branches and subsidiaries. By 1914, for example, the German overseas banks had 53 branches in Latin America alone.[16] Another sub-category was the family-owned and managed merchant banks such as Rothschilds, Barings, and Hope and Co. which had been established earlier but now achieved a level of prominence.

Perhaps the most interesting category, however, consisted of investment banks set up in the 1850s and 1860s specifically to arrange finance for capital importing countries such as Turkey, Sweden, Italy, Egypt, Spain, Russia and the Latin American republics. Often promoted by other banking institutions who sold stock to individual investors, these new ventures were supposed to introduce European capital and project expertise into countries which represented, according to the prospectuses, the wave of the future.

A typical structural pattern involved a branch or home office in London to tap the sterling interbank and capital markets, and business development offices in countries such as Turkey, Egypt, Latin America and the US. Among the survivors of this era were institutions such as Rothschilds and Barings with an effective overseas credit information network, usually in the form of family ties abroad. While Barings, for example, required Bank of England assistance in 1890 because of its holdings of unsaleable Latin American bonds and heavy commitments in Russia, its lending and placement record in the US was excellent, in large part due to its good sources of credit information and conservative lending policies by which the bank was 'not carried away by the excitement of the times'.[17]

In an atmosphere reminiscent of the competition in the late 1970s for mandates to raise syndicated bank loans for sovereign borrowers, these universal banks often appeared more concerned with the earning of arrangement fees than the creditworthiness of the borrower. Generous underwriting and placement fees – the Swedish Government paid Hope and Co. up to $9\frac{1}{2}$ per cent flat for one loan[18] – were augmented by earnings from the deposited proceeds plus capital profits hopefully earned from selling the bonds at a higher price than the discount at which they were purchased from the borrower. In the view of one observer: 'any government which claimed sovereignty over a bit of the earth's surface and a fraction of its inhabitants could find a financial agent in London and a purchaser for his bonds'.[19]

Today's project financing experts would probably be appalled by the quality of feasibility studies for railways built in the four corners of the earth but which were nevertheless able to raise 100 per cent finance in fixed rate debt floated in Europe. European investors looking for higher yields than those available in London or Paris appeared undeterred by periodic waves of defaults which occurred when refinancings could not be arranged because of economic and political problems. In 1873 and 1874 alone, Turkey, Egypt and Spain, as well as half a dozen Latin American governments and roughly half of the US railway companies, defaulted on their foreign obligations. The impact of such defaults on the banks themselves varied substantially, not only as a function of the banks' discretion in choice of borrower but also, presumably, as a consequence of their relative skill and judgement in off-loading their commitments on outside investors. The record of the great majority of the newly-formed investment banks in the 1860s is particularly dismal. The Crédit Mobilier in France, perhaps the prototype of the new institutions, collapsed after an existence of fifteen years during which it launched a variety of subsidiary banks and railway projects throughout Europe.[20] Economic depression, mismanagement and an underestimation of the problems of launching a major project in developing countries all contributed to its demise. Overseas branches of the European universal banks, however, tended to fare better than subsidiaries or joint venture institutions which tended to be less closely controlled by the parent.[21]

One expert estimates that more than half of the several hundred new international banks set up in the boom period between 1856 and 1865 eventually proved abortive, while perhaps one-quarter of the total were insolvent within five years.[22] A sad litany of loan losses, defaults by sovereign entities, inadequate management and foreign exchange losses brought down such creations of the 1860s as the Union Bank of England and France, Continental Bank Corporation, the Anglo-Italian Bank and the Madrid Bank.

US BANKS AFTER THE FIRST WORLD WAR

A final phase of international banking history of interest to today's manager is the expansion of US banks abroad in the period between the First and Second World Wars. Encouraged by the rise of the dollar as a leading international currency, the increase in US corporate investment abroad, and the passage of the Federal Reserve Act in 1914 which facilitated overseas banking expansion, US banks set up networks of branches and subsidiaries abroad for the first time. Their principal objective was to finance US foreign trade and investment, particularly with the Latin American commodity producers, and for the first time dollar acceptances and letters of credit became widely used. From 26 foreign offices and branches at the end of 1916,

US banks had 181 such operations abroad by the end of 1920.[23] Of the latter, 81 belonged to five foreign banking corporations, which foreshadowed today's consortium banks in their multiple ownership by US financial institutions.

The 1921 recession and sharp post-First World War drop in commodity prices, which had previously supported a large portion of the US banks' loans in areas such as Latin America, was certainly a factor in the credit losses and consolidation phase which took place subsequent to 1920. But other factors also lay behind the drop in US bank offices abroad from 181 in 1920 to 107 in 1926 and the liquidation or sale of all the consortium-owned foreign banking corporations. The familiar problems of inexperienced management, excessive expansion and competition for business are regularly cited in accounts of this period. As Phelps pointed out, 'the expansion was unduly rapid and unwarranted; trained men for the management of foreign branch banks were lacking.... They lowered rates, incurring the antagonism of native institutions, and granted credit upon anything but sound bases.'[24]

Chastened by the problems of lending to developing countries and volatile commodity prices (which collapsed again in the early 1930s and brought further losses to banks active in Latin America), US banks turned in the late 1920s to European countries such as Germany, which was then regarded as a first class credit. Acceptance credits were offered to German and Austrian banks until, in March 1931, Germany represented 40 per cent of all US short-term claims on foreigners.[25] Beset by the problems of the Depression and the 1931 banking crisis, the German banks could not roll over these credits and a standstill agreement, which froze the credits, was reached. The extent of the US banks' international commitment at the time was indicated by the estimate that 90 US banks were involved in these standstill arrangements.[26] In the decade prior to the Second World War, a classic work-out took place with periodic partial repayments, conversion into local currency which could be sold at a discount or converted into real assets, and write-offs of the balance.

With the benefit of perfect hindsight into this debacle, one observer blamed competition: 'each lending country operated on its own without apparent regard for the loans and credits showered upon the central European borrowers by their rivals in other countries'.[27] One defender of the banks in a US Senate investigation offered some of the time-honoured justifications of banking behaviour: 'we were perfectly justified in following the example of ... England ... and ... Holland, who in proportion to their resources, gave larger short term credits to Germany than America did. .... It may be locked up for a while, but that is the ordinary risk of business.'[28]

Perhaps the overwhelming impression from this admittedly fragmentary and often superficial view of historical patterns is that very few, if any, of the key issues faced today by international bankers have never graced a Board agenda before. Inexperienced and fraudulent management, the influence of greed in credit decision-making, the problems of lending to sovereign borrowers, over-concentration of lending, inadequate control and guidelines from home office, foreign exchange losses stemming from an inability or unwillingness to obtain cover, and the vulnerability of any international banker to political and economic forces beyond his control – all these problems are as relevant today as they were hundreds of years ago. Today's environment, which involves the support and regulatory controls of central banking institutions, as well as better communications and management information, is undoubtedly different, but the key factors involved in management survival and success have not changed significantly over the centuries.

3 The Internationalisation of Banking: Challenge and Response

By the early 1980s the internationalisation of banking had reached the point at which it was extremely difficult to differentiate between the domestic and international aspects of a bank's wholesale or corporate business.

Factors such as the breakdown of traditional geographic and functional barriers, the growing concern with profit maximisation and the opportunities offered by the Euro-markets as a vehicle to achieve incremental profits have brought hundreds of banks from dozens of countries into the international banking mainstream. In the view of many observers, this internationalisation is a manifestation of the global trend away from retail towards wholesale banking prompted by cost inflation, the rising cost of deposits and other factors.[1] Banks ranging from large US money centre institutions to medium-sized banks from developing countries have 'gone international' for a variety of reasons which form an almost predictable pattern:

(i) a variety of constraints–regulatory, competitive, economic stagnation, physical size–on the profit potential of the bank's traditional domestic market;
(ii) a perceived need to be competitive with other banks in servicing specifically the international needs of traditional corporate customers and generally being seen to be a progressive, competitive bank;
(iii) the desire to broaden and cheapen the cost of funds from money market sources;
(iv) the ability to add substantial incremental profits from assets placed in the international market without incurring significantly higher risks or costs.

The internationalisation pattern which has emerged can be likened to a life cycle which is summarised in Table 3.1.[2]

	Stage 1 Foreign Department	Stage 2 'Going international'	Stage 3 Multinational	Stage 4 Global bank
PRODUCTS	Trade finance, foreign exchange	Syndicated loan participation, trade finance, foreign exchange	Management of syndicated loans, trade finance, foreign exchange	Specialist lending with sectoral risk, cash management, advisory, intermediation. Selective approach based on relative attractiveness
MARKETS	Traditional domestic market	Domestic market plus passive approach to others through loan participation	Major overseas markets in which vehicle is located	Selective approach on global basis depending on relative attractiveness
CLIENTS	Existing domestic clients – a passive response	Existing and new clients from domestic market	Multinationals and others based in overseas markets in which vehicle is located	Segmentation approach to sovereign, multinational, national and retail markets
NETWORK	None	Opening of first offshore office for funding	More offices in major overseas markets	Rationalisation and specialisation
ORGANISATIONAL STRUCTURE	Geographic or functional. Low visibility	Higher visibility; aggregation of functions to international department	Beginnings of functional/customer split	Matrix restructuring to focus on client or product
PROFITABILITY	Minimal	Increasing share – say 5-10% of total; profitability a secondary consideration	Significant share – say 25-35% of total. Concern over relative profitability	Focus on customer or product rather than 'international' profitability

TABLE 3.1   The International Banking Life Cycle

With few exceptions–primarily the handful of British Colonial and American banks which already had major international networks by the 1960s–banks have moved from a passive 'foreign' department stage where they simply responded to the demands of traditional customers to a second stage of 'going international' in which true overseas risks are taken and the banks set up their initial overseas funding operation. From this stage many embark on a further expansion phase to become a 'multinational' institution operating in a number of major overseas markets. The final stage is one where banks large or small become more highly selective and focused in their strategy so as to improve their risk/reward performance. The following chapters will analyse in more detail how this evolution takes place.

ORIGINS AND DEVELOPMENT OF THE EURO-MARKETS

The essential vehicle for the internationalisation of wholesale banking is the Euro-currency market. It was this vehicle which permitted domestic banks to obtain incremental Euro-currency funding, add attractive portfolio assets and develop new banking techniques and products. While other relatively unregulated international banking markets have existed in individual cities in the past, such as Antwerp in the sixteenth century and the sterling market in London in the period until the First World War, the Euro-currency deposit and lending markets are historically unique in terms of physical size, number of participating banks, worldwide scope, and importance not only to bank profits throughout the world but also to the smooth functioning of the international monetary system. The core of the Euro-currency markets is a broadly based and efficient interbank market dealing in offshore-owned deposits and foreign exchange which provide a significant portion of the lending base for the typical bank with an international activity. Based in London and using the US dollar as its principal currency, the market now functions in other centres, from Bahrain to Singapore, and includes most of the currencies employed in international finance. Closely tied to it is the syndicated loan market, where term loans at a floating rate of interest to government and corporate borrowers are syndicated by telex and telephone to the hundreds of banks around the world interested in adding to their portfolio of international assets. Around these have grown up primary and secondary markets in fixed and floating rate negotiable instruments such as Euro-bonds, bank certificates of deposit, and floating rate notes. While several of these markets are based on non-bank investors and participants, international banks are active in them as a manager as well as underwriter and participant.

The twin concepts of an unregulated interbank deposit market in an international financial centre and of international loan syndication among these banks are not new,[3] but what is historically unique is the extent to which the Euro-markets have become a critical structural element in the forward calculations of hundreds of banks throughout the world, most of which had no significant business outside their borders until the Euro-currency markets developed in the late 1960s and early 1970s. Behind the early development of the markets were the internationalisation and rapid growth of corporate business following the Second World War, the availability of vast amounts of US dollars supplied by the US current and capital account deficits of this period, and the various attempts by national authorities in the US, Germany and elsewhere to regulate monetary conditions in their national markets, which encouraged the flow of funds to and from the unregulated offshore Euro-currency markets.

More recently, added stimulus to growth has been provided by the role played by private financial institutions in channelling the massive international funds flows stemming from such recent developments as the increase in the world price of oil, the recession of 1974–5 and the rapid industrialisation of the developing world. With these financing requirements well established, an increasing number of banks throughout the world have become aware of the profit and growth potential of an international deposit and lending function. Whereas until the early 1970s most national banks regarded the Euro-currency markets principally as an opportunity to attract or lay off surplus funds in the context of their domestic business, the constraints on profitable banking expansion in most national banking markets since the 1974–5 recession have impelled an increasing number of banks with little previous natural business abroad to look to the international markets to sustain overall profit and asset growth. The relative ease of entry for a reputable national bank or its affiliates and the ability to add assets and liabilities without the long development period typical of national banking markets clearly facilitated such a decision. Banks which established overseas branches for domestic funding purposes in the late 1960s, therefore, found themselves actively engaged in lending these funds to foreign multinational and sovereign risk borrowers when the domestic requirement disappeared.

The impact of these successive stimuli is vividly demonstrated in Tables 3.2 and 3.3. Table 3.2 plots the physical growth since 1972 of the gross and net Euro-currency market as defined by the Morgan Guaranty Trust Company. The former includes all foreign currency liabilities of banks in major European countries, the Bahamas, Bahrain, Cayman Islands, Netherlands Antilles, Panama, Canada, Japan, Hong Kong and Singapore; the latter nets out claims on banks within this market area. What is unique is not only the physical size of the market, which dwarfs most national money supply totals, but also its steady and consistent quarter-to-quarter expansion. In none of the nine years listed in the table did year-to-year growth drop below 16 per cent per annum; the latter rate was achieved in 1975, the year following the greatest crisis of confidence known in international banking following the Second World War. This growth

TABLE 3.2   Growth of Gross and Net Euro-currency Market (amounts in $ billions)

	Gross		Net	
	Amount	% increase	Amount	% increase
1972	210	—	110	—
1973	310	50	160	45
1974	395	25	220	38
1975	485	23	255	16
1976	595	23	320	25
1977	740	24	390	22
1978	950	28	495	27
1979	1220	28	615	24
1980	1515	24	760	24
1981	1800	19	890	17

Source: World Financial Markets, Morgan Guaranty Trust Co.

has taken place despite repeated forecasts of a likely shrinking or actual collapse of the market as a result of factors such as the removal of US exchange controls, the crisis of banking confidence in 1974 related to the collapse of the Franklin National Bank and Bankhaus Herstatt, and periodic disappearances of OPEC surpluses.

To exploit this global market structure, there has been an unparalleled proliferation of new overseas units–representative offices, branches, subsidiaries and affiliates–as well as the steady rise in the number of banks opening their first overseas office. US institutions have led this surge: from roughly 100 offices in 1951, the number of foreign branches of US banks had risen to a level of 803 at the end of 1981. A total of 157 US banks were operating overseas branches by December 1981.[4]

Banks from other countries have responded to the challenge of the American banks' entry into their traditional markets as well as the profit opportunities revealed by this penetration. British banks moved in the 1970s away from their traditional dependence on semi-autonomous affiliates to acquire control of existing overseas banks and set up new branches. German institutions, after losing their extensive international network on two occasions after the two world wars, have largely rebuilt their structures. Whereas only three German overseas branches existed at the end of 1963, a total of 87 branches and 56 subsidiaries were in operation by the end of 1981.[5] Similar overseas growth has been shown by banks in France, Japan, Canada and other major Western countries.

The net result of this proliferation of overseas vehicles is shown in Table 3.3 which lists the number of foreign banks and their operating vehicles in 26 major financial centres.

Whereas the first surge of overseas expansion took place in the major international and national markets such as London, New York, Hong Kong and Tokyo, Table 3.3 reveals the extent of the second phase: exploitation of individual national markets such as Korea and Venezuela which are perceived to offer particularly attractive profit prospects. The relative unattractiveness of interest differential lending in the form of syndicated loans to major international borrowers led many banks in the late 1970s and early 1980s to focus on clients based in these national markets.

The impact of this remarkable international expansion is

TABLE 3.3   Foreign Banks Represented in 1981 in Major Banking Centres[a]

Centre	Number represented[b]	Number of operating vehicles[c]
London	389	269
New York	194	167
Frankfurt	156	61
Singapore	155	116
Hong Kong	148	154
Paris	130	94
Luxembourg	124	113
Tokyo	121	57
São Paulo	113	35
Bahrain	110	77
Sydney	97	28
Grand Cayman	92	106
Jakarta	86	30
Los Angeles	80	67
Nassau	78	98
Caracas	78	11
Beirut	73	41
Mexico City	73	4
Zurich	71	48
Toronto	71	32
Brussels	67	50
Buenos Aires	66	24
Rio de Janeiro	64	22
Manila	58	33
Chicago	58	38
Seoul	51	32

[a] Source: *Who is Where in World Banking,* The Banker Research Unit. All centres with 50 foreign banks or more are listed.
[b] Includes banks with common interests in consortium bank or representative office.
[c] Includes agencies, OBUs, branches, subsidiaries and consortium institutions with foreign ownership.

reflected in the available data showing the extent of foreign penetration of individual national banking markets. In September 1981 the US offices of foreign banks held 13.6 per cent and 18.9 per cent respectively of total US banking assets and business loans.[6] In the UK 16.5 per cent of the banking system's sterling advances at the end of 1981 were made by non-British institutions.[7] Foreign banks in Japan, however, accounted for only 3.5 per cent of the total loans and discounts made by all banks at that point in time,[8] while in February 1982 foreign branches in Germany were responsible for only 5.1 per cent of loans by commercial banks to non-banks.[9]

What has been more unexpected is the movement overseas of non-US banks, many of whom vowed as late as the mid-1970s that they did not need branches abroad, that the Euro-currency market was unreliable and unstable, and that they had no interest in doing business internationally with any but their existing domestic customers. A growing number of national banks, therefore, has come to regard the international market as a desirable target in its own right. While their natural preference is for a domestic or existing customer, they are now prepared to look at international lending opportunities on their own merits and not simply as an appendage of their basic domestic business. As a result, the international market has reached a level of self-sustaining growth which includes an element of self-fulfilling prophecy, because as more banks develop purely international operations in anticipation of a growth in this market, the latter in fact does grow, if only because the new entrants have made their contribution. Whether a new representative office or branch, the physical opening of a new business development outlet creates significant human and institutional pressures for that office to add new business for the group.

The most recent phenomenon has been the internationalisation of banks from a variety of developing countries. Such institutions look to the Euro-markets as a reliable source of funding for their domestic business as well as a means of asset diversification. Another characteristic of newcomers to the Euro-markets is the relationship of international banking to the evolution of a wholesale/corporate banking function. A number of retail-oriented institutions – savings and co-operative banks and their central institutions, regional banks and others – have perceived their future to lie in wholesale banking, and they approach international banking as an extension of this focus on corporate clients.

THE ROLE OF COUNTRY RISK LENDING

One of the dominant characteristics of the internationalisation of banking is the essential role played by country risk lending, which can best be defined as credit exposure in an overseas country where there is some degree of perceived risk that foreign currency will not be available to meet public and private sector obligations. In a typical bank's early stages of international development, such risk was limited to short-term credit extended to prime overseas banks in the context of financing trade flows.

As the bank's client needs and its own desire to build an incremental base of profitable assets began to drive its international strategy, this exposure became longer term, represented a much larger portion of the total balance sheet and related to a much wider range of overseas public and private sector borrowers. Having set up an international deposit and lending structure, banks found that the biggest game in town was lending to sovereign entities which had vast requirements for balance of payment support loans. The coincidence of the banks' desire to add profitable assets and indirectly satisfy client needs with balance of payment funding requirements thus created a vast new market for credit products.

The importance of country lending is summarised in Figures 3.1 and 3.2. The former plots the overall growth of new syndicated Euro-currency loans together with the proportion of loans made to private non-bank borrowers during the period 1973–81. The latter figure, while not an ideal measure of loans to private sector corporate entities, does serve as a useful proxy to show the relatively dominant role played by loans to government entities and financial institutions which are usually government-controlled.

Figure 3.1 thus points up the apparent inconsistency between the publicised reason usually given by banks for going international – to follow their domestic customers – and the actual result – a loan book which is usually predominantly sovereign risk in nature. The inconsistency is explained by the relatively small direct demand for credit by private sector corporate clients and the latters' understandable desire to use a friendly bank to support their efforts to invest and sell products abroad by assuming the ultimate overseas risk.

By the early 1980s, however, the absolute and relative burden of foreign debt had become a major concern to international banks. In the mid-1970s conventional banking wisdom considered loans to sovereign entities as virtually riskless in view of

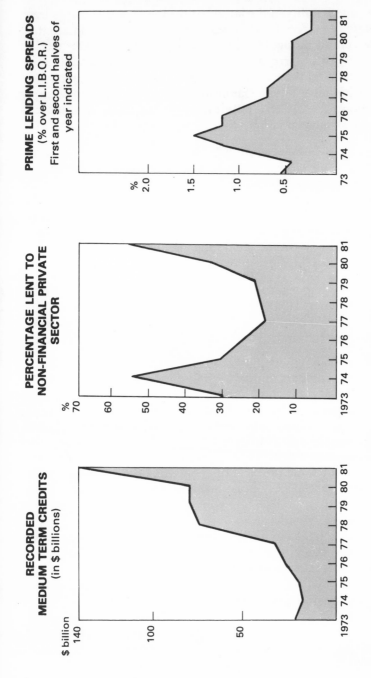

FIGURE 3.1   Euro-market Trends, 1973–81

Source: O.E.C.D., Salomon Brothers.

the presumed ability of the latter to take the necessary measures to allocate resources for debt servicing in order to maintain the country's credit rating. Having just gone through a major world recession with a corresponding number of corporate failures, bankers satisfied themselves with the knowledge that there was no US Chapter 11-type bankruptcy procedure for sovereign governments. A Citicorp publication perhaps best summarises these comfortable assumptions:

> Private banks must approach the question of a developing country's debt-service problems on the basis of (1) the funda- mental distinction between the developing country's debt to *official* creditors (governments and official international fi- nancial institutions) and debt to *private* creditors; (2) the assignment of the highest priority to servicing the private debt; and (3) the fundamental assumption that debts to private banks must be serviced as scheduled.[10]

Successive shocks to banking confidence during the late 1970s and early 1980s in the form of debt reschedulings in countries such as Turkey, Sudan, Nicaragua, Poland and Mexico shattered this rationale. It became apparent, for example, that:

(i) Countries could indeed mismanage their affairs to the extent of being unable to realise the potential of undoub- tedly substantial natural resources;

(ii) Internal political pressures could be such that a govern- ment could not survive if it were to divert the necessary foreign exchange to debt service;

(iii) The level of debt was becoming so high in some cases that the inevitable political or economic problems – war, civil strife, commodity price declines, etc – necessitated a re- scheduling of debt, often on terms involving an economic loss to the banks;

(iv) Private banks in a rescheduling exercise could not realis- tically expect preferential terms *vis-à-vis* multilateral or public sector lenders and were thus likely to suffer the same economic loss as had the latter in earlier reschedulings;[11]

(v) The level of debt service was so high that even a moderate shift in bankers' confidence levels was sufficient to bring about the self-fulfilling prophecy of an inability to attract new funds from the banking community;

(vi) Private bank lending practices exacerbated country debt management problems by withdrawing credit lines, shifting to short-term exposure, and continuing to lend even when a country manifestly required a debt restructuring.

Figure 3.2 shows graphically the deterioration over the 1971/2–1981 period of the debt service ratios of the principal non-oil non-Comecon LDCs. While no single ratio can effec-

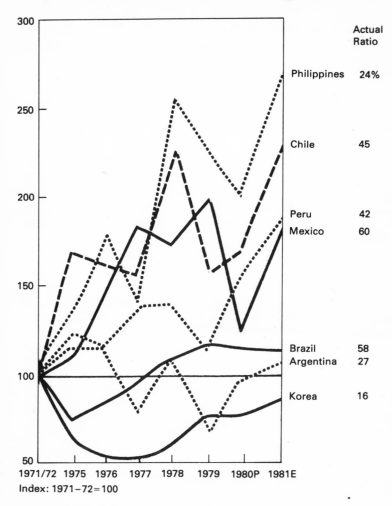

FIGURE 3.2   Debt Service Ratios: 1971/2–81

Source: World Bank.

tively measure the ability of a country to service its foreign currency debt, an analysis of this ratio over time represents a useful approximation of the inability of major developing countries to increase their foreign-source revenue at the same rate as their foreign obligations.

FUNCTIONING OF THE EURO-CURRENCY MARKET

A dominant feature of today's Euro-currency market is its efficiency in the broadest sense of the term. This efficiency is reflected in a positive sense in the ability of an acceptable bank in normal times to raise fairly substantial sums from other banks in a matter of minutes at market rates. In addition, the technique of marginal pricing through the use of the London Interbank Offered Rate for given maturities eliminates for the lender the possible squeeze in margins which can occur with the use of an administered rate subject to political influence such as Base Rate in the UK and prime rate in the US. As will be discussed subsequently, management may choose not to match its loan rollover and deposit periods, but in normal circumstances the lender does not have to take an interest rate risk on his loan portfolio.

Other variables in the lending function have either been eliminated or reduced to standard formulae. While Euro-currency loan agreements can provoke a few violent arguments, the points at issue are usually few and far between. With few exceptions, therefore, the key variables in negotiating a Euro-currency loan have been reduced to maturity and pricing. The variable of currency, for example, has been controlled by covenants limiting the borrower's option to currencies such as dollars, Deutschemarks and Swiss Francs which can be raised fairly easily from the deposit or foreign exchange markets. Non-US banks have traditionally been concerned about their ability to attract dollar deposits to fund Euro-currency loans, but overall market liquidity since 1974 plus the proliferation of foreign branches and agencies in the US would appear to have significantly alleviated this potential problem.

By potentially limiting such variables, however, this efficient market has led to an increasingly homogeneous and well-defined product, which in turn has resulted in a more intense level of competition than would have been the case with more product differentiation. On the lending side, the great majority of syndicated loans – principally sovereign risk credits – are marketed to participants essentially by telex, which presumes a fairly straightforward yes-or-no credit decision; only rarely does a bank's credit function have to pile through reams of statistics to sort out the risks involved. Loan terms are precisely defined by a highly efficient pricing mechanism; for most borrowers at any given time in the market, the informed lender can immediately quote the 'right' maturity and loan spread, give or take ⅛ per cent in rate or a year in maturity.

This relative lack of product differentiation intensifies the existing degree of competition which stems from the steady increase in the number of market participants and the growing pressure on them to show continued growth in international earnings and assets. With several hundred international banks looking for business, it is much easier to cut prices on a standardised product than it would be for a specialist one where only a limited number of competitors are prepared to understand and bid for the business. The oft-mentioned tendency for Euro-lending to swing naturally towards a borrower's market thus reflects a combination of an increasingly homogeneous product and a larger number of participants interested in increasing their international exposure.

Another by-product of the efficiency of the market of vital interest to management is the crucial question of confidence. This characteristic is, of course, by definition an integral factor throughout the world in the banking sector; virtually no level of liquidity or capitalisation will protect a bank from its depositors if, rightly or wrongly, they are convinced that their obligor is unsound.

This is even more true of Euro-banking, where a greater portion of deposits is obtained from the potentially more volatile money market than is the case domestically, and where rumours can spread with the speed of a telephone call. Moreover, the time disparity between final loan maturity and average life of deposit – and, therefore, the potential liquidity gap – is perhaps higher in the Euro-currency market than in any other. This so-called transformation of short-term deposits into long-term loans is clearly one of the structural weaknesses of the international markets.

The crisis of confidence which struck the international banking community in 1974 after the Franklin and Herstatt failures came very close to a domino-like collapse of the Euro-currency market by cutting off the supply of funds to smaller and newer banks, which in turn could have led to a broader freezing of assets and liabilities. Given this market characteristic and the absence of an agreed international lender of last resort, it is understandable that international bank management does everything in its power to maintain its market reputation as well as secure backstop funding arrangements. For a period of time in 1974, a variety of otherwise viable banks were faced with the choice of funding their loan book with shorter maturities than they would have wished, paying a premium rate for funds or using the backstop funding facilities of parent or related institutions.

Eight years later, increased market tensions in 1982 stemming from concern over credit quality brought about a recurrence of differential pricing, or 'tiering' of the interbank deposit market.

Another reflection of the efficiency of communications in the market is the tendency of international banks to imitate the behaviour of those regarded as leaders. Whether it involves a new organisational structure, setting up in a new financial centre, or developing a specialist expertise or product, one can be certain of a wave of imitators as the market followers struggle to keep up with the innovators. Once a newcomer to the ranks of international borrowers is accepted in the form of a successfully placed loan, he can be sure of receiving the visits of a variety of bankers who had studiously ignored him previously. By the same token, if word gets around that a market leader has a negative view on a particular sovereign borrower, the latter will have some explaining to do to anxious lenders to maintain its name in the market.

CHALLENGES FOR THE INTERNATIONAL BANKER

The challenges posed by the evolution of the Euro-currency market represents only a few of the problems raised by the environment in which international banks operate. Figure 3.3 summarises seven environmental factors which establish the

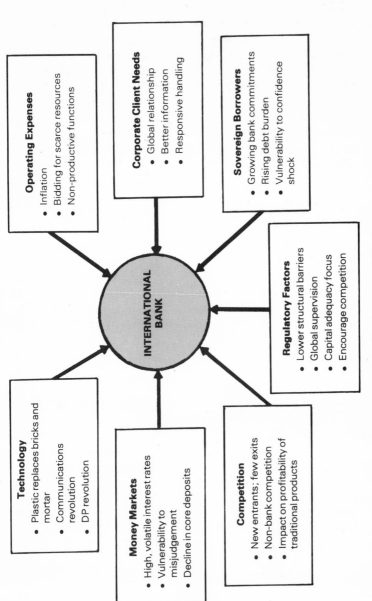

FIGURE 3.3 Environmental Challenges

Source: DIBC.

framework within which the international bank manager must plot his strategy.

(i) *Competition:* the analysis above has described a market characterised by low barriers to entry, psychological exit barriers, relatively undifferentiated products, and a resulting deterioration of the risk/reward ratio in credit-based products, the core activity of most international banks. An indication of the pressure exercised by new entrants is provided by Figure 3.4, which tracks the number of banks during the period 1972–80 which have appeared in the 'tombstones' advertising syndicated Euro-currency credits.

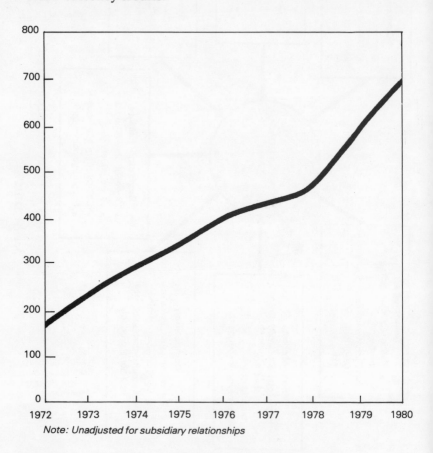

Note: Unadjusted for subsidiary relationships

FIGURE 3.4   Number of Euro-lenders Identified in Syndicates

Source: Office of the Comptroller of the Currency.

(ii) *Increase in operating costs:* international banks have been subjected to the same inflation-induced increases in unit expenses as many other businesses. Perhaps more important, however, is the impact of several factors peculiar to international banking. The first is the need in a highly competitive market to bid for scarce resources: specialist personnel such as experienced sectoral lending officers and software programmers; prime financial district sites for offices, and the like. Secondly, as a bank expands its international network, what was originally a simple one-office wholesale banking operation manned by a few dozen in staff is now a multi-unit network requiring a variety of expensive but non-revenue generating staff or management functions: regional headquarters personnel, auditors, country risk economists, automated systems for risk control and international personnel specialists.

(iii) *Risk of loss on sovereign loans:* the perception of increased risk in loans to heavily borrowed sovereign entities has been described previously. Traditional credit assessment techniques have been applied to sovereign lending with limited effectiveness, and the influence of political factors on heavily indebted borrowers has increased the unease with which banks attempt to evaluate individual country risks.

The prospect of extensive reschedulings with the possibility of loss of interest or principal has implications for the quality of banks' loan portfolios as well as the possible need to revise strategies built on such lending. Even a substantial upward movement of lending margins would be insufficient to compensate for a loss in economic value comparable to that suffered by official lenders in past reschedulings.

(iv) *The impact of technology:* developments in computer and communications technology are having a revolutionary impact on internal bank control systems, branch networks and the ability to process transactions. Retail banking throughout the world is the principal focus of this revaluation in terms of replacing bricks and mortar, full service branches with plastic card and other automated payments systems.

Wholesale banking is affected as well in that a variety of functions – deposit taking, F/X and money dealing, and others – may not require a physical presence in a given market centre. Coupled with the seemingly inexorable rise in operating costs, these developments are causing banks to rethink their delivery systems strategy.

(v) *Regulatory influences:* the two major trends in regulatory policy in the early 1980s have had a significant impact on international bank strategy.

On the one hand, regulators throughout the world are concerned about banks' capital adequacy and the ability of banks to generate sufficient earnings internally to maintain capital ratios in the face of expanding balance sheet volumes. Figure 3.5 shows the steady deterioration of the capital:assets ratio for

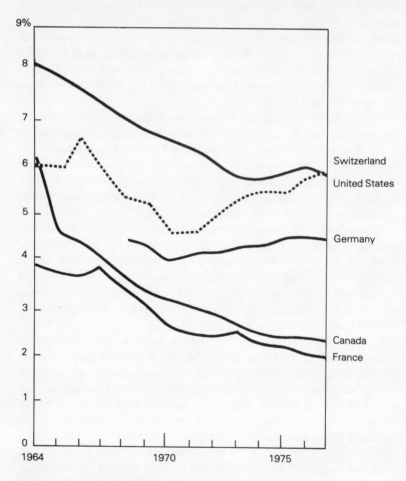

FIGURE 3.5   Capital Adequacy Ratios

Source: OECD (Professor J. R. S. Revell).

banks in key countries since 1964. Such deterioration has been avoided in a few countries – principally those such as Germany and Switzerland where there exists a statutory requirement to maintain a given ratio.

On the other hand, regulators in many countries are supporting the reduction of artificial barriers to competition so as to create a more efficient financial structure. Barriers to entry by foreign banks have thus come down in countries such as Spain, Finland, Korea and Canada with a corresponding impact on the profitability of traditional banking products. Within individual countries such as the US, regulators are eliminating artificial limits on interest rates, geographic market positions, and the range of permitted services.

(vi) *The requirements of corporate clients:* most international banks give top priority to the client segment of multinational corporations. Such firms generally have a highly centralised and sophisticated financial management, specialised requirements throughout the world and a determination to obtain their banking services at highly competitive prices.

Quite apart from the need to protect an existing relationship from the depredations of competitor institutions, banks have found that the level of financial expertise represented by these clients is often equal to or superior to that of their own international banking officers, who are more at home in dealing with other bank or sovereign institutions. Moreover, the often centralised approach to financial decision-making in these firms places at a disadvantage banks organised on a territorial basis with an account officer who may or may not have an understanding of international finance. Thus, while corporate clients – particularly those with a base in the bank's natural market area – represent a logical target in terms of understandable credit risk and interest in a variety of banking products, servicing their needs at a profit represents a major challenge to most banks.

(vii) *The risk/reward of treasury mismatch positions:* the international banking community has gradually adjusted to the current environment of rapidly fluctuating interest rates and currency parities. Given the pressure to maximise profits – particularly without burdening the bank's balance sheet – there is a correspondingly high motivation to take interest rate and currency positions. While some banks have outstanding records of success in such a strategy, the growing sophistication of an increasing number of players in these markets and the persistence of apparent anomalies such as reverse yield curves has raised the level of risk in such trading activities.

With such an extensive array of problems posed by his external environment, today's senior international banker faces challenges which did not exist in the straightforward banking market of the 1950s and 1960s. Such a senior manager probably achieved his position by virtue of performance in lending money successfully or developing new business; today's managerial challenges may thus require a different type of skill. The balance of this book will explore how management has reacted to such challenges.

4 Articulation of Objectives and Strategy

This chapter will examine first the conceptual approach used by consultants and certain banks to articulate their international strategy. It will then discuss the actual practice of how banks' strategies have evolved over different developmental phases and how banks actually approach strategic issues.

THE CONCEPTUAL APPROACH

While bankers – like so many managers – instinctively feel that their business is totally different from any other, a conceptual framework for strategic analysis has been developed in the 1970s and early 1980s by a number of international banks working alone or with outside management consultants. In view of the growing acceptance among banks of the need for such a framework to enable a bank to achieve its goals, Figures 4.1 and 4.2 have been provided to illustrate an approach which might be taken. The strategic planning process described in this chapter can be defined as an integrated set of actions to achieve a sustained competitive advantage.

Figure 4.1 portrays a typical international bank planning framework. Three basic inputs are required:

(i) An evaluation of the external environment along the lines of the analysis in Chapter 3;
(ii) An assessment of the bank's internal strengths and weaknesses: the bank's culture and risk preference; the existing products, markets and client relationships; its financial and human resources; overseas network and domestic alternatives;
(iii) The bank's overall objectives: financial goals, client service, community obligations, working environment, and so on.

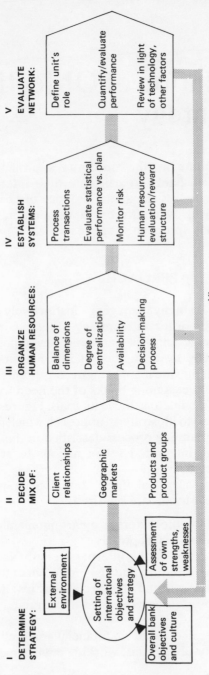

FIGURE 4.1   The Strategic Process

From this analysis should emerge a statement of the bank's international mission, or overriding goals, as well as possible strategies designed to achieve these goals. These strategic options in turn revolve around choices made in the three dimensions in which an international bank's activity can be analysed:

  (i) *Geographic markets:* national or regional market places such as the UK, Latin America, or the Comecon countries;
 (ii) *Products or groups of products:* individual products (such as letters of credit, syndicated loans, F/X advisory services) or groups of related products (trade finance, merchant banking, Treasury services);
(iii) *Client relationships:* these can be broken down or segmented by category – sovereign entities, multinational corporations, medium-sized national firms, wealthy individuals, and so on.

Figure 4.2 is a three-dimensional diagram showing the interrelationships of a typical client/product/geographic matrix.

Having evaluated the relative attractiveness in terms of

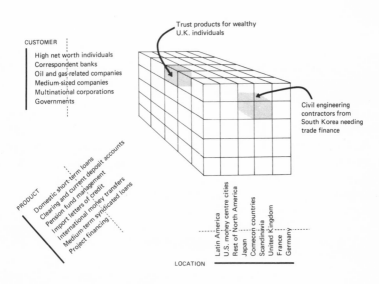

FIGURE 4.2   Matrix Relationships

growth and profitability of each possible product, client or market opportunity, the bank can then complete its strategic analysis by evaluating the implications of such options in terms of:

(i) Organisational structure and decision-making processes: what type of organisation and structure will be required;

(ii) The ability to attract/develop/retain the necessary human resources;

(iii) The delivery system or vehicle network required;

(iv) The financial and physical resources necessary to carry out the programme in terms of present capital adequacy, ability to tap additional capital and generate internal profits and other factors.

The next step is to select the optimal strategy in terms of appropriateness to the stated objectives and the realities analysed above. Once selected, the strategy is implemented by a series of long- and short-term business plans, monitored by the appropriate plan – actual comparative data, and executed by staff throughout the organisation who are given specific, measurable tasks and rewarded on the basis of their performance.

HOW BANKS ACTUALLY ARTICULATE STRATEGY: AN EVOLUTIONARY PROCESS

One of the dominant characteristics of international bank strategy is its evolution over time as strategy becomes driven by different forces. While there are many individual deviations from the pattern described below, and while factors such as a bank's size and level of corporate banking sophistication have a major impact on the timing and form of this evolution, the broad outline of this evolutionary process is typical of most banks active today internationally.

While senior bankers have, in one form or another, addressed each of these aspects of strategy formulation in the process of developing their international business, it is relatively rare to find a thoroughgoing and comprehensive strategy established at the outset. More typically a bank has simply responded to such specific challenges and opportunities as a competitive threat, a profit opportunity, the leadership of an aggressive member of senior management or the international department, the demands of traditional customers and the psychological need to be seen to be active in a growing market populated by competitors. As the international function grows, more systematic efforts are usually made to define specifically where the bank is going internationally and how it will get there.

To a very large extent, the relative lack of strategic thinking in a bank's early expansionary phase reflects both the background of senior international bankers and the traditions which have, until fairly recently, characterised the banking industry. Until the 1960s when a few American banks began to regard their business as simply another industry whose ultimate objective was to maximise long-term profitability to the stockholders, banking was a heavily regulated, utility-type sector which existed to safeguard customer deposits, intermediate these deposits into secure, self-liquidating and high quality loans and fixed rate investments, maintain sufficient liquidity to meet depositors' needs, and provide the banking services required by retail, corporate and government clients. Relations with other banks tended to be co-operative rather than competitive, and management success tended to be measured in terms of quality of assets and service as well as continuity and reliability. The relative focus in many countries since the mid to late 1960s on profitability as the ultimate goal of the bank has obviously upset this pattern, and international banking with its relative newness and its significant profit potential has particularly felt the resulting emphasis on competition, profit performance, need to establish an identity and differentiate products and other factors which were relatively unimportant in earlier years.

International bank management itself has reflected this transformation of objectives, style and performance criteria. Traditionally, senior international bankers had risen in the corporate hierarchy on the basis of proficiency and success in dealing with other banks, in providing a specialised service such as foreign exchange or in general knowledge of the international scene. With the new emphasis on profits and the need to compete to obtain these profits, other skills assumed greater importance: corporate lending experience, skill in creating and marketing new products, management information and data processing expertise, and the personnel skills needed to manage a multinational staff throughout the world became vital considerations.

Perhaps most important were the management skills required to organise and direct this rapidly evolving and growing international structure.

The exceptions to the evolutionary pattern described below tend to be the handful of banks which were active internationally well before the Second World War – some of the larger US institutions and those with old colonial ties to countries such as Britain and Holland. Whereas the great bulk of today's international banks began their evolutionary process in the 1960s and 1970s, this limited number of US and 'colonial' banks with extensive networks were already multinational in character by this time.

(i) *Phase 1: the passive foreign department:* Table 4.1 describes briefly the initial stage of international development, when the international function of a national bank was a service department responding fairly passively to the needs of domestic and overseas customers and representing a very minor portion of the bank's overall staffing, assets and earnings. Services offered normally related to trade finance – collections, letters of

TABLE 4.1   Phase 1: The Passive Foreign Department

STRATEGY	an operating function passively processing domestic clients' needs
PRODUCTS	trade finance (documentary credits, money transfer, F/X execution, travellers cheques, collections, etc.)
CLIENTS	traditional domestic corporate and retail
MARKETS	home market
OVERSEAS NETWORK	none except possibly retail branches abroad
TREASURY	any Euro-funding handled by domestic treasury function
ORGANISATIONAL STRUCTURE	geographical structure dominates; overseas lending and treasury may not be included in international; low status
PROFITABILITY	relatively unimportant
NATURE OF INTERNATIONAL RISK	short-term bank-to-bank; otherwise domestic risk

credit, the provision of foreign exchange – and overseas customers tended to be primarily foreign banks with whom correspondent relationships in individual overseas countries were established. The human skills required at this stage of a bank's
international development were those of a generalist and di-
plomat as well as technical knowledge of foreign trade transactions and the movement of funds internationally. In its role as a
passive service organisation dealing primarily with other banks,
the international function was thus usually well removed from
the mainstream of a bank's corporate deposit and lending
operations. Organisationally, because of this factor and the
relatively small profit contribution made by his function, the
head of international was rarely a key member of his bank's
senior management team. While the appellation of 'Foreign' or
'international' Department was clearly a geographic designation, in most European and other banks it was effectively a
functional one as well in that it provided specialist services
rather than operating as a 'bank within a bank'.

There was no overseas wholesale banking network, and any
international or Euro-funding was handled by the home office
treasury function. Risks were essentially domestic in that traditional customers usually assumed any credit risk other than the
usual short-term exposure associated with correspondent bank
credit facilities.

(ii) *Phase 2: 'going international':* the strategy drivers for the
second phase, which is described in Table 4.2, are the perceived
need to compete for existing clients' international business
together with a growing concern over the limitations on domestic profit growth. The internationalisation of traditional corporate clients' own business is expressed in requests for an international banking capability which are received positively by bank
management concerned about a variety of threats to their
existing domestic banking franchise.

A major thrust of this second phase is the active solicitation of
prospects as well as existing clients in the bank's domestic
market. The prospects of building, at a low overhead cost, a
diversified portfolio of international assets yielding a contractual and presumably assured spread over the cost of funds leads to
the first significant overseas medium-term exposure in the form
of participations in syndicated Euro-currency loans. Short-term
foreign bank credit risk now is supplemented by medium-term

TABLE 4.2   Phase 2: Going International

STRATEGY	driven by growing international needs of existing clients and perception that these will otherwise be met by competitors; perceived limitations on domestic market
PRODUCTS	trade finance; more active F/X positioning; portfolio of syndicated loan participations
CLIENTS	active solicitation of traditional domestic clients
MARKETS	domestic market plus experimentation with others through loan participations
OVERSEAS NETWORK	first wholesale unit opened in major financial centre
TREASURY	overseas unit establishes embryonic international treasury; F/X and deposit positions taken
ORGANISATIONAL STRUCTURE	higher status; outside recruitment; more delegation of authority
PROFITABILITY	still low % of total – perhaps 5–10%; market positioning has priority over profits
NATURE OF INTERNATIONAL RISK	prime sovereign, corporate and bank medium-term risks through loan participation

exposure to a variety of overseas sovereign or private sector borrowers without the guarantee of a domestic client.

At this stage, an international treasury function begins to emerge. While a foreign exchange function may have existed in the form of a correspondent nostro (own account) balance which could be used to meet a customer's currency requirements, a new dealing function might be set up to operate directly in the market and, in addition, take currency positions for the bank's own account. The need to diversify or expand sources of money market deposits for essentially domestic purposes – particularly in countries with controls on domestic lending – would lead to the establishment of an initial foreign branch or subsidiary, often a 'brass plate' operation which functioned with little or no autonomy as a funding arm of the parent organisation.

Having established the bank's name in the Euro-currency markets as a taker of deposits primarily for domestic purposes, an obvious next step was trading deposits to earn matched and mismatched profits on the interbank or redeposit book. Another approach might involve participation as a minority partner in a consortium of preferably like-minded institutions to test the international water and minimise the commitment of staff and other resources.

During this stage, profitability is a poor second priority to the perceived need to establish oneself as a fully competitive international bank. On the other hand, in organisational terms the international function increases in absolute importance; senior experienced staff may be recruited; and greater delegation or new authority in areas such as credit and treasury may be granted to the international function.

(iii) *Phase 3: the multinational bank:* in phase 3, the goal of maximising profitability begins to drive strategy. The concern to be competitive with peer banks leads to a growing and substantial commitment of the bank's earning assets to the international function, while a network of overseas units is established in major banking centres. Table 4.3 also points up a broadening of the client and product base in this phase: locally based corporate and other clients in markets such as the USA and UK where new operating units have been opened and higher value-added products such as the arrangement of syndicated loans or the establishment of a specialist lending group in a product area of perceived natural strength and attractiveness. The treasury function now comprises a variety of local currency funding operations along with Euro-currency trading in most of these centres. The need to co-ordinate and control the latter eventually leads to some form of a global treasury structure.

In organisational terms the international function now comes closest in many countries to being a 'bank within a bank' with its own funding, credit, staff, network and other capabilities. By the same token, this creates strains both internally and externally, where it becomes more difficult to mesh the marketing of international and domestic products to a corporate client who requires a global service relationship. Initial steps are therefore

TABLE 4.3 Phase 3: The Multinational Bank	
STRATEGY	profitability begins to drive strategy; management perceives need for more sophisticated, higher value-added strategy in variety of target markets
PRODUCTS	trade finance, F/X, arrangement/co-management of credit facilities, beginnings of specialisation in lending
CLIENTS	locally based sovereign and private sector entities in target markets where a vehicle is located
MARKETS	limited number of major world financial centres and national markets plus traditional market
OVERSEAS NETWORK	operating units or offices in 'major financial centres'
TREASURY	local currency funding in these centres; beginnings of a global treasury function controlling local units
ORGANISATIONAL STRUCTURE	initial appearance of functional and client orientation as specialist and multinational groups set up; problem of global service to corporate clients
PROFITABILITY	international now represents major portion – 25 to 35% – of total; growing concern about return on international capital/assets
NATURE OF INTERNATIONAL RISK	exposure to locally based firms; treasury now a profit centre with higher risk level

often taken to break down the traditional international/ domestic distinction on a functional or client basis by setting up a specialist lending group (for example, energy, shipping) or carving out a multinational or corporate group which handles specific multinational clients.

The international function now represents a major portion of the bank's total earnings and assets, and concern for relative profitability becomes the dominant management concern. Various efforts are made to calculate international profitability as a basis for allocating resources; while these involve making some heroic assumptions on allocating revenue and expense categories, most indications are that domestic banking produces a higher return on assets and shareholders' funds. The bank's risk profile is now multinational with growing direct exposure to overseas-based corporate and government entities, while treasury has become a significant profit centre based on deliberate deposit and F/X mismatch positions in a number of currencies.

(iv) *Phase 4: the global bank:* a limited number of international banks have reached phase 4: that of the global institution, whose principal traits are described in Table 4.4. At this stage, the profitability goal has obliged management to take a totally

TABLE 4.4	Phase 4: The Global Bank
STRATEGY	focus, selectivity and pragmatism now characterise strategy as profitability becomes dominant goal; financial strength, existing network and domestic alternatives determine breadth and depth of bank's global reach
PRODUCTS	focus on higher value-added, fee-based products derived from systems and expertise
MARKETS	selective approach to identify higher profit potential markets anywhere in the world where competitive advantage can be obtained
OVERSEAS NETWORK	rationalisation of existing network
TREASURY	global treasury management with tendency towards centralised control
ORGANISATIONAL STRUCTURE	matrix organisation with client/product/ market dimensions; global account relationship officers
PROFITABILITY	concern with profitability of individual markets, clients and products rather than 'international' as a whole
NATURE OF INTERNATIONAL RISK	specialist sectors; interest rate exposure management now critical

pragmatic and focused approach to each of its products, markets and clients.

From this analysis have emerged a number of banks – the larger US, UK, Canadian and a few other institutions – with a global reach in terms of a very broad spectrum in each of these dimensions together with a correspondingly large overseas network. A much larger number of banks have evolved a more limited spectrum of products, clients and markets in which they believe their competitive advantage can be translated into an acceptable level of profitability. Whatever the size of the bank or extent of its global reach, however, the common elements of phase 4 are the analytical process undertaken and the conclusions drawn from it as to allocation of resources.

In product terms, there is a focus on expertise and systems-based products which add significant value and generate fees which are not directly related to credit exposure. A segmentation approach to clients analyses categories such as sovereign entities, multinationals, national or middle-market corporations, high net worth individuals and the general retail market. Individual country markets are evaluated in terms of profit and growth potential as well as the bank's ability to develop a competitive advantage.

The overseas network which emerges from this analysis is based on the client/product/market mix chosen. Given the profit constraint, this usually involves a restructuring of the network built up in phase 3: closing and merging of units, specialisation or rationalisation in others, and the opening up of a few more in target markets. The treasury function has now become a global one with centralised control of risk and profit in home office or a major offshore centre.

Organisationally, the distinction between domestic and international has been replaced by one based on client (retail vs. wholesale) or product grouping (merchant banking vs. commercial banking). A global account relationship officer is responsible for bringing to bear product and geographic expertise within such a matrix organisation. A bank's management information system is now geared to produce profitability and risk data on individual clients, products and markets rather than the international function as a whole. Risks taken by the bank become equally focused: speciality lending sectors, target clients, and specific national markets.

OBJECTIVES AND STRATEGY: RESPONSE TO QUESTIONNAIRES

The categorisation outlined above is admittedly arbitrary. It does, however, provide a conceptual framework within which the great majority of international banks have evolved in the 1970s and early 1980s.

In an effort to define more precisely how banks set objectives and define strategy, the author has conducted two broad surveys of senior international managers. The initial one, carried out in mid-1978, is described in detail in Chapter 1 and was designed for the first edition of this book. The second was undertaken in late 1980 for the American Bankers Association and involved interviewing approximately 100 bankers in US and non-US banks operating in ten countries.[1] The former was structured in that responses to specific questions were quantified; the latter was unstructured and concentrated on understanding the bank's international strategy and its choices of products, clients and markets. Both surveys suffer from the obvious limitations on a banker's willingness to discuss his competitive strategy with an outsider, but the process of in-depth questioning combined with a study of actual behaviour does enable the analyst to draw some useful conclusions.

In the case of the first questionnaire, the inconclusive responses when aggregated were often attributable to inclusion of banks in markedly different phases of strategic evolution, whereas a segmentation by peer group – US money centre banks, Japanese City banks, German Landesbanks, and so on – would produce much more definitive and consistent responses.

In the 40-bank survey, it was apparent that relatively few banks had elaborated and communicated internally a well-thought-out set of international objectives ranked in terms of priority. Profitability and service to customers are the two most frequently cited objectives, a ranking which reflects the increasing profit orientation of banks throughout the world as well as the oft-expressed view that banks are in business primarily to service their customers' requirements.

Of the 33 banks in the survey which were prepared to express a priority, roughly three-quarters stress profits, while for the remaining quarter servicing existing or new customers is the top priority. A slightly higher percentage – 80 per cent – of the

North American banks cited profits as their principal objective; only 58 per cent of the other institutions took the same view. The same emphasis on profitability is reflected by cumulating the top three objectives expressed by the bankers. Profitability and service to customers were cited by all but a few banks as two of their three principal objectives. In quantifying their profit objectives, most banks refer to a target percentage of total bank earnings or portion of the balance sheet represented by international business. Interestingly enough, less than one-third of all the banks interviewed felt that meeting competition was one of these three top priorities. A few banks believe that furthering their country's national interests is a valid priority objective, while others referred to improving the quality of service, increasing the extent of diversification, maintaining market share, and providing a full range of services.

In some of these cases, it can be argued that strategies are being confused with objectives. Many, for example, pointed out that effective servicing of customer requirements permits banks to achieve their profit objectives and that the two are inextricably linked together in the real world. It can also be argued that such objectives, which are generally incorporated in some form of annual planning process, do not necessarily reflect the actual priorities pursued in practice. Profit maximisation is undoubtedly a very real objective for virtually all banks, but the relative importance of service to customers as an *objective* can be disputed. While the provision of banking services which are hopefully of high quality and reflect a relatively unique approach is undoubtedly of great importance to international bankers, this presumed objective is often articulated to the outside world as an acceptable justification for a decision which is motivated in reality by other objectives such as profitability, diversification of risk, expansion of market share, etc.

Responding to competitive pressures and increasing market share are, on the other hand, goals which are often cloaked under what are assumed to be more acceptable objectives. Banks which, for example, have the largest single share of a given national banking market are unlikely to broadcast the fact that one of their principal objectives in expanding internationally is to retain that prized position. Recognition of reality is also a factor in the setting of priorities; one US bank has deliberately established customer service as its top priority as it recognises that in the current market it cannot demonstrate superior profit performance to the domestic banking function. Another rarely articulated but highly relevant objective is the offsetting of domestic profit shortfalls. Many banks plagued with unexciting domestic earnings – or, worse, significant domestic loan losses – have deliberately used international business as an accordion or buffer to offset these shortfalls; when domestic earnings recover, correspondingly less emphasis is placed on international business.

Although most bankers have thus established profitability and service as long-term objectives, relatively few institutions communicate them throughout their organisation and attempt to quantify or articulate them in the type of detail which lends itself to an effective overall planning process. American, Canadian and British banks are fairly specific about their profit and other objectives, whereas at the other extreme, Japanese and Southern European institutions tend to rely on implicit, fairly general statements of objectives.

There is some degree of correlation, however, between the relative importance of the international function and the specificity of objectives. Large American banks, for example, have relatively well articulated objectives, but it can also be assumed that other institutions come under considerable internal and external pressure to justify their use of resources when the latter approaches one third or more of total assets or income. In such circumstances long-term profitability is perhaps the most logical justification for the claim on resources, whereas in a small or less internationally-oriented institution, a relatively implicit, defensive commitment to serve existing customers will suffice as a *raison d'être* for the international function. For banks such as US regional and Japanese institutions, however, as the international function expands considerably to provide such services, incremental profitability is increasingly called upon to justify the substantial commitment of resources.

The responses by senior international bank managers in mid-1978 to questions relating to strategy selection reflect essentially their approach to obtaining a competitive advantage rather than any choice of product, client or market. They also track the position of the individual bank in the strategic evolution from the passive stance of phase 1 to the more articulated and focused approach of phase 4.

Of the 25 banks responding to the specific question, speed/flexibility of the decision-making process and specialist expertise were each mentioned by about one-quarter of the banks as representing the single most important facet of their long-term strategy. Another quarter mentioned quality of service or unique products and services as their highest priority strategic element, so that if one assumes that quality of service is equivalent to a specialist function, the largest number of banks, roughly one-half, focus on some form of product or service differentiation as their principal competitive weapon. No other specific strategic approach was mentioned by more than 15 per cent of the bankers.

If one evaluates these responses by combining the three highest priorities ranked by the respondents, speed/flexibility of decision-making was by far the most frequently mentioned competitive strategy (by 28 banks). Another 17 banks gave specialist expertise as one of the top priorities, 16 mentioned the existence of a large existing customer base and 13 cited the ability to commit relatively large amounts of funds. If one lumps together those citing specialist/unique/high quality expertise, the resulting figure of 27 banks is comparable to the number focusing on speed/flexibility of response. The most significant difference in response between North American and other banks is the relative emphasis by non-US and Canadian instituions on the priority of a large existing customer base. This would appear to reflect the relatively defensive objectives of many European and other banks in protecting their customer base from the assault of US institutions and the latters' relative lack in many cases of such a base.

At the risk of over-generalising, therefore, it would appear that the typical international bank defines its strategy in terms of finding some degree of product or service differentiation and emphasising its ability to provide a quick and constructive response to customer requirements. In practical terms, banks look to their natural strengths – domestic industry, geographic location, market share, existing services – to 'find a niche' or otherwise differentiate themselves from their competitors. Larger banks can be expected to explore market opportunities on a fairly thoroughgoing and comprehensive basis to select their targets and priorities, whereas smaller institutions tend to rely on existing skills and specialities to achieve the desired level of differentiation. As will be discussed in a subsequent chapter, however, customers may well disagree both as to the responsiveness of the decision-making process and the extent to which a given bank's services are truly unique or superior to those of the competition.

Of almost equal interest are the possible competitive strategies which ranked lowest in the respondents' priorities. Only five banks, for example, mentioned fineness or competitiveness of pricing as one of their three priority competitive elements. This reflects traditional attitudes towards the use of pricing as a competitive factor; few banks want to see themselves as deliberate price cutters. In the real competitive world, however, such a strategic element is often necessary for survival, as is emphasised in the level of loan spreads in the late 1970s and early 1980s, as well as the responses given by chief financial officers as described in a subsequent chapter. The priority given by so many banks to the responsiveness of their decision-making process might well reflect a desideratum or objective, more than a strategic means, in view of the widespread criticism, particularly of the larger banks, as to the time necessary to receive approval for a given commitment.

Another possible competitive factor which received relatively little emphasis is the offering of unique products and services, which was mentioned as a priority by only six institutions. The vast majority of the bankers interviewed were quite pessimistic about their ability to introduce and profit from such new products in view of the highly competitive nature of the market and the difficulty of developing a product or service which was truly innovative.

Banks outside the US were those who placed a particularly high priority on their ability to commit large amounts of funds and on the possession of a large existing customer base. Once again, at the risk of over-generalising, a typical European or Japanese bank would appear to place a great deal of strategic emphasis on its ability to commit large amounts of funds on an expeditious basis for an existing customer which it knew well. American banks, on the other hand, seem to rely more on product differentiation and the geographic coverage of their world-wide network as well as the speed and flexibility of their decision-making process to win business.

Another factor in the setting of strategy is the relative urgency of pressure to achieve given objectives. Banks which have a substantial amount of natural business stemming from their location or historical ties, or who effectively control the business of their domestic customers, naturally have less incentive to elaborate a detailed strategic plan involving significant product differentiation. The importance of the profit drive to strategy articulation is thus a function not only of position on the banking 'life cycle' but also of the relative ease with which a bank can earn an acceptable return on its existing business.

APPROACHES TO MARKETING

As international banks become more concerned about strategic differentiation, their approach to marketing has changed significantly. In the traditional 'foreign department' stage, bankers considered themselves as purveyors of services required by customers and lenders of short-term funds to finance trade, at the request of such customers, on a virtually risk-free basis. Other international banks were collaborators and sources of useful business.

In line with the traditional approach of using foreign correspondents as a source of business, banks originally attempted to market their services through these correspondents. Over time most banks found that their competitors were picking up this corporate business, either directly or through more persuasive solicitation of the foreign correspondent bank. Another approach in the late 1960s and early 1970s involved minority participations in joint venture or consortium operations with a variety of objectives in a number of overseas locations. With few exceptions, these institutions were found to be inadequate as marketing channels because of the difficulty in establishing the identity of the parent institution through a common vehicle, which was often having a sufficiently difficult time in establishing its own marketing presence.

Having tried a variety of indirect marketing approaches, most medium and large-sized international banks by the mid-1970s became convinced that direct marketing by their own officers was the principal means of establishing their marketing identity and therefore the basis for selling their products. Given the advantage of a physical presence in overseas markets, a bank's representative office, branch and subsidiary network was, therefore, a logical selling force in these markets.

By the mid-1970s, therefore, most international bankers had come to realise that they had to compete to achieve their profit and other goals, and that competition in the financial markets meant dealing with the elements of marketing: determining who the customer was, what the customer wanted, developing products and services to meet this demand, pricing these services to meet the competition and provide for a satisfactory return, and developing the appropriate channels through which they were to be sold. While marketing as a concept is now more acceptable to bankers, there is still a residual view that marketing is both unbankerly, in that it is not correct or professional to sell one's services, and unnecessary, in the sense that traditional relationships and quality of product are sufficient to do the job. Many banks have created internal marketing functions or hired outside marketing experts in an effort to come to grips with the problem, but by and large marketing concepts as practised in industry have not significantly penetrated the thinking of senior bankers. On balance, however, the impact of competition and the increased sophistication of corporate customers have obliged banks to think more seriously about product development and product differentiation. Chapters 5, 6 and 7 explore in more detail the three critical marketing dimensions of product, market and client relationship.

5 Products

The range of products and services made available by international commercial banks has evolved in response to the changes in strategic direction described in Chapter 4. Table 5.1 provides a list of typical products which such a bank might offer as it moves away from traditional deposit and lending products towards higher value-added, fee-based services. Such a listing is not, of course, relevant for universal banking institutions in Germany, Switzerland and other countries.

In its early stages of international development, a bank's products are essentially those required by its wholesale and retail clients in connection with international trade and investment: the movement of funds across national borders, making available foreign currencies and the extension of credit in various forms. At this point in time, it is rare for the bank to think in terms of well-defined, specific products which can be priced, marketed and evaluated on a stand-alone basis. The bank is simply offering a range of related services which are required by its clients and correspondents, and it is the overall relationship which is vital to the bank.

Two forces, however, lead to a broadening and sophistication of a bank's international product line. The growing emphasis on profitability and competitive pressures on the return from traditional deposit and credit products encourage banks to offer products which provide a higher yield by virtue of their greater value added or higher level expertise. Concurrently multinational and other corporate clients are demanding more sophisticated products in the form of more efficient and comprehensive cash management systems, knowledge of a variety of international financing mechanisms and global banking relationships.

In the category of credit products, the response takes the form of more sophisticated or complex forms of extending credit: taking a project risk rather than lending 'against the balance sheet'; syndicating a large performance guarantee or direct credit rather than simply extending credit on a single-bank

TABLE 5.1 Product Options for International Commercial Banks

Category of product	Traditional commercial banking	Higher value-added fee-based services	Possible non-banking diversification
		Development phase	
CREDIT	Letter of Credit Overdraft and other short-term credit Term lending Guarantee Acceptances	Project Finance (Shipping, Energy, Aerospace, etc.) Export credit schemes Performance L/C Syndicated lending	Underwriting/Trading of quoted Securities Insurance Underwriting
DEPOSIT/FUNDS TRANSFER	Custody Payments clearing Deposit-taking Payments/funds transfer Lock box Collections Travellers cheques	Proprietary payments systems money transmission, plastic cards)	Payments/clearing utility
INTERMEDIATION & ADVISORY	F/X trading for client account Credit information	Third party funds management (Liquidity, Securities, Portfolio, Pension Trust, etc.) Financial advice (Project Management, Mergers and Acquisitions, Capital Restructuring, Tax Advice) F/X Advisory Service Raising of Non-Bank Finance (Currency Swaps, Private Placements)	Securities brokerage Management Consultancy Recruitment Insurance Brokerage Venture Capital Sale of Software Packages

Source: DIBC.

basis, and arranging a multinational export credit scheme rather than simply handling the local currency facility.

The dominant theme of the trend to higher value-added credit products is the emphasis on earning fees rather than simply adding risk assets which are of declining attractiveness in an environment of growing concern about capital adequacy. While the successful marketing of such more sophisticated products usually does produce higher fee revenues, efforts to maximise these revenues often conceal the fact that the fee earned is simply a proxy for an extension of credit which in logic should be included in the capital adequacy calculation. This is true of guaranty and letter of credit fees as well as acceptance commissions; it is somewhat less true of loan syndication fees when the bank is taking a significant share of the credit on its own books.

In the area of deposit and funds transfer products, major banks have developed highly automated cash management systems enabling correspondents and corporate clients to obtain faster credit for funds, better information on the status of these funds and, in some cases, the ability to initiate transactions without the bank's intervention. Concurrently there is a trend towards the 'unbundling' of such products and the charging of fees for specific services rather than relying on compensation from deposit balances yielding less than market interest rates.

The revolution in communications and computer technology offers considerable scope for such services, but the high cost of developing such new products and the possible shrinkage of the core deposit base render their future profitability somewhat problematical.

The intermediation and advisory products being offered by international commercial banks represent the most direct effort to penetrate the market usually associated with investment/ merchant banks, securities houses and universal banks. Some of these fee-earning activities, such as portfolio management advice, have traditionally been carried out by commercial banks in their domestic activities. More importantly, the latter believe they can exploit their existing corporate client relationships and financial expertise to market a range of financial advisory, non-bank credit and third party funds management products. The success of German and Swiss universal banks in marketing such products strengthens the determination of commercial banks to overcome traditional and legal barriers such as the Glass Steagall Act in the US.

The 1978 questionnaire indicated a broad desire by banks in non-universal banking countries such as the USA, Canada and UK to develop a capability in both the intermediation/advisory products described above as well as securities underwriting and trading. Of the 39 banks responding to the question, only six (15 per cent of the total) felt that diversification beyond the commercial banking sector was not particularly desirable. All but one of the non-North American banks interviewed supported the universal banking concept, while three-quarters of the US and Canadian institutions, which are restrained domestically from investment banking activities, agreed.

On the other hand, the rationale and strength of feeling among the latter banks varied considerably. Some expressed a very lukewarm and experimental desire to expand their range of services and were clearly uncomfortable in doing so. Many were frank to admit that their rationale for expanding into investment banking activities was either purely defensive or motivated by the need to exploit another market now that their traditional sector of activity had become so competitive. By the same token, those with relatively undeveloped domestic or international commercial banking potential were correspondingly unexcited by the glittering prospects of fee earnings from investment banking services. The very largest banks without an investment banking tradition, however, tended to be the greatest advocates of diversification, given their objective of maximum market coverage.

Many commercial banks have grouped high value-added, fee-generating products into a merchant banking or special services organisational category reflecting the nature of the skills required to develop the market and provide the services. The organisational implications of such a decision are discussed in Chapter 11.

A number of large international banks intend to move well beyond these higher value-added products into a third group which can perhaps best be described as non-banking products, most of which fall in the category of other financial services. For such banks, the profit potential of both investment/merchant and commercial banking products is seen as limited, and the broader financial services sector offers not only attractive profit opportunities but also the opportunity to cross-sell a variety of products such as insurance underwriting and brokerage, securities underwriting and brokerage, computer software and a retail payments system through plastic cards.

The desirability and feasibility of new product development is the subject of great debate among international bankers. Most bankers accept that their principal product is money which is fungible and whose pricing in recent years has been a function of competitive forces rather than perceived risk or the need to obtain an adequate return on funds at risk. Rather than increasing product differentiation and development, international banking competition in the 1970s and 1980s has actually reduced it in many respects through increasing uniformity in the pricing of Euro-loans and the use of standard loan agreements. Successful new lending techniques such as the concept of pricing loans at a floating rate over the cost of funds and the medium-term negotiable floating rate note (FRN) and floating note CD(FRCD) have, in effect, been introduced into the market, but the rapid adoption of these techniques by competitors has made it extremely difficult for the innovator to retain any sustained financial benefit.

For most international banks, product development consists of adopting and/or perfecting existing products already marketed by other banks or financial institutions. A limited number of institutions – principally the larger US banks – are committed to the investment of funds in truly new products such as automated cash management or letter of credit systems.

Even these banks recognise that new products, however successful, are unlikely to modify significantly a commercial bank's basic dependence on interest differential income from lending activities. For such banks, the positive impact of a new product on the bank's image is likely to exceed the benefit to its bottom line profit performance.

For the great majority of banks, however, new product development carries a much lower priority than the need to market existing products more effectively, to offer a responsive and flexible service and to upgrade the skills needed to offer these products on a professional basis.

The pricing of international banking products has become largely a function of competitive factors rather than the conscious fixing of a price to reflect credit risk, return on invested

TABLE 5.2 International Department Gross Revenue Classified by Services Rendered

International Banking Service	Percentage Contribution to International Department Total Gross Revenue for 40 US Banks*						Mean	Range
	0%	1–10%	11–25%	26–50%	51–75%	76–100%		
Export Credits and Trade Financing	11	11	6	6	5	1	20.7	0–86
Lead Bank or Originating Bank Lending	16	9	2	7	4	2	20.6	0–87
Participation in Syndicated Loans	12	14	6	5	2	1	14.9	0–79
Eurodollar Trading	21	8	6	5			9.7	0–50
Letters of Credit	1	33	6				5.8	0–20
Foreign Exchange	2	31	7				5.6	0–24
Acceptances	5	29	6				5.2	0–23
Retail Services Abroad	38	1		1			0.8	0–29
Merchant Banking	39			1			0.8	0–30
Other	11	18	4	2	1	4	15.9	0–94
							100.0	

* Five banks did not provide this information.
Source: Center for International Banking Studies.

funds or coverage of expenses. Fees and margins on credit products in the borrower's market which characterised most of the 1970s and early 1980s have essentially been determined by the desire of the marginal lender to obtain the business – interrupted, from time to time, by concerns over a particular borrower's credit-worthiness. Dealing spreads, advisory fees and various usage commissions are also determined in large part by competitive considerations. One of the most aggravating aspects of an international banker's job is the conflict between his professional judgement as to the correct pricing of a credit facility and the real world impact of competitive considerations.

The breadth of a bank's international product line, as expressed in the oft-repeated claim of offering 'a full range of services', has traditionally been a high priority for senior management. The logic of cross-selling a large number of products to a single client or correspondent is reinforced by market studies which emphasise a multinational's preference for the convenience of such a global banking relationship. Analytical studies generated by pressures to maximise profitability, however, have pointed up the low return on many traditional products, and many banks are being forced to choose between these two often conflicting goals.

In recent years, a number of studies have attempted to quantify the importance of specific international banking products. These efforts have been handicapped by the inclusion of banks at widely different stages of development which tends to blur otherwise sharply defined product patterns. One useful study was carried out in 1979 by the Center for International Banking Studies in the USA which analysed the gross revenue contribution by product group of 40 US banks.[1] Table 5.2 summarises the results, which highlight the importance of lending products as well as the wide range of percentage contributions for each product category. For the mean bank, however, the first three credit products listed accounted for 56.2 per cent of international revenue.

Another useful survey was that executed in late 1981 by the Group of Thirty.[2] Table 5.3 summarises the responses of 111 international banks which were asked the following question:

Which of the following aspects of international banking business are currently significant activities for your bank?

TABLE 5.3   Significant International Activity

Which of the following aspects of international banking business are currently significant activities for your bank? (Please check the lines that apply.)

Activity	All Banks per cent
Foreign exchange	90
Servicing overseas needs of domestic customers	89
Direct lending to multinational companies	78
Participation in syndicated Eurocurrency loans	73
Lead management of Eurocurrency loans	60
Other special services	53
Investment banking	45
Local currency lending in overseas markets	45

Source: Group of Thirty.

This sample is substantially broader than that of the earlier study and does not attempt to quantify the importance of each product group in relative terms. It does, however, point up the widespread importance of foreign exchange as well as credit products.

6 Markets

The selection of individual overseas markets and the approach to such markets is an integral element of an international bank's strategy. As in the case of products and clients, an evolutionary trend is clearly visible as banks throughout the world prioritise markets, determine what – if any – vehicles are appropriate to exploit these markets, and evaluate the sovereign risk associated with lending to borrowers there.

When a bank initially approaches the issue of which markets to enter, the dominant consideration is usually participation in the money market and Euro-loan syndication activities of a major international financial centre. The objectives of unrestricted access to the Euro-currency deposit and F/X markets, proximity to the Euro-loan syndication market, and the international credibility that comes with an overseas operating presence thus dictate an initial overseas unit in a major centre such as London, New York, Luxembourg or Hong Kong. The choice of one of these centres is largely a function of cultural and business ties, geography and the location chosen by peer banks. What is being selected is the international dimension of a given market-place rather than its local aspects, which may be of interest to the bank at a later phase of its development.

The second phase of a bank's market expansion is the opening of banking units in a number of priority countries. These markets are selected on the basis of such factors as the trade and investment patterns of the bank's clients, perceived importance of the local economy, geographic spread and a variety of subjective factors peculiar to the individual bank. Thus Japanese banks open branches in countries with major trade ties to Japan, Spanish banks place a high priority on Latin America, American and other banks wish to be established in major national economies such as Germany and France, and Western European banks desire a Far Eastern presence in Tokyo or Hong Kong.

Concurrent with this second phase of development is the

decision, at least on a selective basis, to develop direct relation-ships with locally based firms rather than rely on traditional correspondent relationships. This can be an agonising decision for those recipients of substantial correspondent banking busi-ness. At the same time, building a portfolio of participations in syndicated Euro-currency loans enables a bank to learn more about a given economy, provide through such familiarity a degree of comfort to the Board of Directors or senior manage-ment, and assist in the selection of markets to be entered subsequently.

The net result of this market expansion phase is the prolifera-tion of banking offices in the major developed OECD countries and offshore markets described earlier in Table 3.3. As foreign banks – initially the major US institutions – in the 1960s and early 1970s entered a new market which had previously been dominated by local banks, their competitive impact produced attractive profits for the newcomers as well as structural change in domestic banking relationships and practices. Techniques and products introduced by US banks – the use of marginal cost pricing, term lending, project finance, the use of a global relationship officer, and so on – gave the newcomers a competi-tive advantage which was translated into significant profits in countries such as the UK, France, Germany and Italy. In other countries, such as Japan, foreign banks were welcomed for the role they played in providing external finance or introducing beneficial change into a domestic banking market.

More recently, these patterns have been visible in countries which have opened their banking systems to foreigners in the early 1980s on a systematic basis – Finland, Korea, Spain and Canada. Often introduced by local regulatory authorities to provide a more efficient financial market-place, foreign banks have attracted profitable local corporate business by introduc-ing new lending and deposit-taking products as well as providing more sophisticated advisory and intermediation services.

Over time, however, the foreign banks' initial competitive advantage diminishes as local banks respond in kind, more foreign banks enter, and local corporate treasurers become more sophisticated and aware of their banking alternatives. Thus, in the major OECD markets, the profitability of the principal lending and deposit products sold to multinational affiliates and major local corporations, which are the principal targets of foreign banks, has been reduced to a common 'international' level almost regardless of the location of the borrower. In 1982, therefore, a highly regarded multinational would be able to obtain local currency or Euro-dollars in countries such as the UK, France, Holland, Germany or the USA at an interest margin of perhaps $\frac{3}{8}-\frac{1}{2}$ per cent over the cost of money market funds for a short- or medium-term exposure.

In these relatively open and sophisticated markets, local banks are matching the techniques and products offered by foreign institutions and demonstrating their competitive advantage through the availability of lower-cost domestic funds, a larger local branch network, and ability to service middle-sized companies effectively. As a consequence, most Western European units of major foreign banks are relatively unprofitable in terms of return on funds employed in the local market and are maintained largely to provide the global capability needed to service multinational corporations.

The attention of major international banks interested in a direct banking presence overseas is therefore focused on a diminishing handful of markets hitherto closed to overseas banks, such as Brazil, the major wealthy Arab countries, Australia and Venezuela. The attractiveness of these markets lies in their growth prospects. While foreign banks may eventually be permitted to enter such markets, it is difficult to see a large number of such institutions benefiting substantially from such liberalisation in view of the relatively small size of most of these markets and the local authorities' presumed determination to prevent an onslaught which might jeopardise the competitive position of the indigenous banks.

As international banks extend the range of markets in which they are active so as to improve their profit performance, they increasingly confront the issue of sovereign or country risk. Whether they operate through a locally based unit or not, by the time a bank has reached its phase 3 'multinational' life cycle phase, it is extending credit to borrowers in several dozen or more countries. For most of these markets there is a generally acknowledged country risk in the sense of some degree of concern as to the country's future ability and willingness to meet its foreign currency obligations. Operating through a banking unit lending local currency may not involve the same concern over foreign exchange availability, but the ultimate success of such a unit is clearly tied to the host country's external credit-worthiness and its ability to repatriate earnings.

Faced with the difficulty of assessing sovereign risk, banks have relied largely on two assumptions in building their exposure to specific markets: diversification of risk and the belief that sovereign governments would manage their economies and external borrowing policies so as to maintain their external credit-worthiness. While diversification through the maintenance of country limits is still a critical factor, the volume of sovereign-related credit needed to achieve a bank's international growth and profitability targets has put severe pressure on such banks to increase exposure to heavily borrowed countries. More importantly, the experience of the late 1970s and early 1980s in Turkey, Zaire, Sudan, Poland, Mexico and Argentina showed how political and economic obstacles to debt service can arise when the burden of foreign debt increases. Whereas in the mid-1970s very few bankers were prepared to admit that there was the prospect of economic loss in the form of loss of interest or principal on a sovereign loan, by the early 1980s it was generally accepted that the prospect of substantial and extended reschedulings had significantly diminished the quality of a typical bank's sovereign loan portfolio.

In a highly efficient market such as the international lending sector, there is a high degree of correlation between perceived risk and reward in lending to entities in countries representing a perceived degree of country risk. Banks motivated by the desire to build a profitable international capability are therefore confronted by a growing concern over country risk as they attempt to increase the level of earning assets in markets which provide a satisfactory reward.

7 Client Relationships

The third dimension of a bank's international strategy is the selection and servicing of client relationships. Through a process of segmentation by which clients and groups of clients are ranked in terms of potential attractiveness and the bank's ability to develop a profitable and growing relationship, an international bank explicitly or implicitly selects the relationships on which its strategy is based.

Figure 7.1 shows the range of possible categories of relationships from which a typical bank might select its own priority groupings.

Sovereign entities (including government-controlled financial institutions), which represent by far the largest category of actual credit exposure for international banks, do not normally rank highly in the latter's strategic priorities. Even if there is no particular concern over sovereign risk, international bankers generally believe that a profitable relationship is relatively difficult to establish with a government entity. While the latter often disposes of substantial deposit funds, these are generally placed at competitive market rates with major banks reflecting the low-risk preference of the depositors.

More importantly, banks find that there is less demand for sophisticated credit and other products from an entity whose primary demand from an international bank is substantial credit at the most competitive rate. To quote one senior banker, 'The only thing you can sell a government is cheaper money.'[1] By the early 1980s the practice on the part of credit-worthy sovereign borrowers of requesting international banks to tender for the management of syndicated loans had become widespread, whereas the demand for sophisticated advisory and intermediation services remained limited. Finally the turnover of political appointees in government entities increases the difficulty of developing long-term business relationships.

On the other hand, a number of the larger international banks have developed strong and profitable relationships with

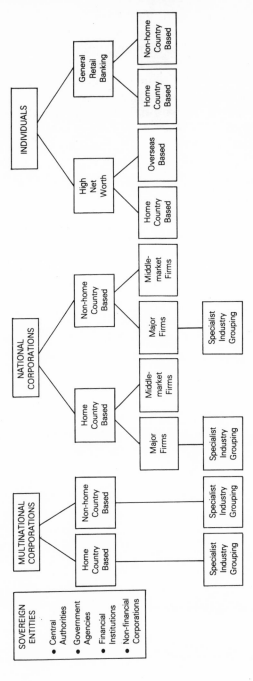

FIGURE 7.1   Client Options for International Banks

Source: DIBC.

sovereign agencies and institutions. Such banks play a preferential role as a depository and lead manager of Euro-currency syndicated loans to the government, and significant fees are earned on advisory and intermediation products related to the management of the country's liquidity and overseas assets.

Multinational corporations – large firms with a major commitment to more than one national market – generally represent one of the highest priority relationship categories for most international banks. Those based in the bank's home country constitute a natural priority in that they often represent the motive force for the bank's international function; it was 'following our clients abroad' which was the bank's initial justification for moving out of phase 1 in its life cycle. Another natural priority category is foreign-based multinationals with operations in the bank's domestic market area. Such clients offer not only the opportunity to provide a useful service in one's home market but also an introduction in other markets in which the multinational is active.

Quite apart from the logic of dealing with firms who have requirements which can be met from a bank's existing expertise and relationship base, major corporations are attractive to banks from a credit standpoint as well. Corporate credit evaluation is a skill with which bankers are professionally comfortable, and the presence of a local operation facilitates credit monitoring. In addition, corporations can make better use of a wide range of intermediation as well as credit and deposit products. Finally, personal relationships with corporate officers are perceived to be more long-standing and productive over time than those with government officials.

On the other hand, these positive attractions are substantially offset in the view of a growing number of banks by the multinational's high level of financial sophistication and insistence on competitive pricing of most banking products. Many of these corporations have a level of financial sophistication in their treasury function which is equal to or superior in many respects than that of many of the banks soliciting their business.

For many multinationals, international banks offer only one interesting product – money – at the most competitive rate. For others, the efficient movement of international funds is critical, with the result that low-cost bank balances shrink. One product of the multinational's sophistication – or negotiating leverage –

is its ability to utilise its cash balances with banks to obtain a variety of services with the result that the net relationship profitability to the bank may be quite unattractive. It is primarily in the more sophisticated credit, deposit and advisory products where a bank can obtain premium compensation from such a relationship.

National corporations represent a third possible client category. For the larger firms, the dividing line between multinational and national is admittedly arbitrary. Most national firms of interest to an international bank will be relatively smaller and less sophisticated internationally than a multinational, and many will fall into the category of 'middle market', a grouping used by some banks for companies with revenues in the range of $5–$100 million equivalent. For analytical purposes, many banks therefore distinguish between middle market and larger firms in a given national market.

National companies may or may not have an international dimension, which would obviously be of interest to an international bank. More important, however, is the lower level of sophistication and perceived credit-worthiness of most such firms, which enable banks to earn a higher reward than in the case of a multinational as well as establish a relationship which it is to be hoped will grow with the client.

Whether the target firm is categorised as a multinational or national corporation, banks often identify specific functional or industry groupings of firms on the basis of common characteristics or speciality requirements. Early in their international evolution, banks may establish a specialist industry grouping on the basis of existing domestic capabilities or perceived market attractiveness. Thus a Texas bank might naturally identify the category of energy clients active both domestically and internationally, while a Norwegian bank could do the same for the shipping industry. As a bank's product line becomes more sophisticated in terms of sector-specific services, additional functional units may be added to handle the perceived requirements of such sectors.

In segmenting the overall category of individual clients, banks distinguish between so-called high net worth individuals and retail clients in general. The former are presumed to require specialist, personalised services for which premium compensation can be charged, while in the latter case convenience and low cost are assumed essential. Although the domestic operations of many international banks are predominantly retail in character, only a handful of them have made a major commitment to retail banking abroad. The obvious obstacles to such a strategy include the high capital and operating costs of providing a retail banking service competitive with local banks, the uncertain future economics of retail banking due to new technology, and the presumed cultural and structural differences between retail markets around the world.

On the other hand, several groups of international banks have identified specific national retail markets which they consider particularly attractive. The most numerous are those providing retail services to large numbers of home country nationals or those with cultural ties to the home country: Japanese banks in California, a variety of banks from southern Europe and the Indian subcontinent in the UK, and Israeli banks in a variety of countries. Another category is a small number of US and Canadian banks which are attracted to selected markets such as the UK which have a perceived high spread between retail deposit and lending rates. Others have acquired local banks with a significant retail business in countries such as the USA.

By and large, however, the rising costs of providing any form of competitive retail banking service abroad have obliged most banks to focus entirely on wholesale clients. An exception is sometimes made for the high net worth individual whose substantial financial resources and/or connections with major wholesale clients justify the provision of a tailor-made service in the form of investment, estate and tax advice. The flow through of higher oil revenues to many individuals from OPEC countries has been a major incentive to give special attention to such clients.

As an international bank's strategy evolves, greater emphasis has been placed on the client relationship as the focal point at which a bank's products and market expertise converge. Behind this trend lie the growing range and sophistication of bank products, the increased number of markets in which a bank might operate, and the insistence by multinational corporations on a centralised, global relationship which matches their own central treasury direction.

Such a tendency has been translated by a growing number of US and other banks into the designation of a single account officer, or relationship manager, who mobilises the bank's specialist skills and products for the client. Whereas in many banks clients must deal directly with the relevant geographic market or product specialist, to an increasing extent he relates in the first instance to a generalist relationship officer who is presumably fully conversant with his requirements and can mobilise the bank's resources to fulfil them.

Each international bank at a given point in time has explicitly or implicitly established priorities among the type of clients indicated in Figure 7.1. With few exceptions, however, there is a subjective and/or objective preference for those based in the bank's home country. The objective preference is based on a likely competitive advantage in understanding and meeting the client's requirements. The subjective preference relates to the greater degree of comfort felt by such constituencies as a bank's board of directors/supervisory board, stockholders, and outside analysts with domestic as opposed to overseas risks. Countless international managers have come to realise that a given loss in lending to a foreign entity is far less well-received by such constituencies than an equivalent loss on a domestic credit. The strength of this subjective preference is often a function of the international experience and orientation of the management. In the banks who are relative latecomers to international banking, the domestic orientation of senior management often seriously limits the flexibility of international managers in selecting client priorities.

MULTINATIONAL CLIENT SURVEYS

Multinational corporations have been the subject of a number of customer surveys because of the priority they represent for the typical international bank and the relative facility with which a broad spectrum of corporate treasurers' views can be obtained. For the first edition of this book, a survey of 30 senior financial officers of major multinational firms was undertaken in 1978 by the author to provide an appropriate context for the discussion of international banks' marketing and business development strategy. The firms which completed the questionnaire attached as Appendix C are located in the US, UK, continental Europe and Asia and represent a small but reasonably representative sample of the heavily solicited multinational corporations which are the declared target of most international banks' marketing efforts.

The questions in the survey focused on the respondents' attitudes towards adding new banks to their list of relationships; their evaluation of existing banking relationships, and what they consider weaknesses in the performance of international banks. While these comments naturally reflect only one side of the banker – customer dialogue, useful conclusions may be drawn from individual comments and some fairly well defined response patterns.

International bankers can anticipate an interested and open, albeit critical, reception when they try to establish an initial relationship with a multinational corporation. Less than 10 per cent of the respondents were unprepared under any circumstances to establish a new banking relationship, while only two of the thirty financial officers actively discouraged initial or 'cold' calls by a bank with whom he did not yet do business. The almost universal attitude is that such newcomers often bring new ideas and approaches to their problems and may represent a useful learning experience, particularly when a company is entering a new market or is dissatisfied with an existing banking relationship. One regional treasurer of a major US multinational firm welcomes the calls of new banks even though his region has existing relationships with 147 different institutions. Such heavily solicited officers try to select out fringe banking institutions and make it clear to the others how difficult it will be to develop an actual relationship. As a senior treasury officer of a major British multinational puts it: 'we try to strike a balance between containing perpetual growth in our banking relationships, but at the same time neither slam the door rudely in anyone's face nor close our minds to the creative thinking that can sometimes be stimulated by a new contact'.

While they thus feel obliged to receive new prospective bankers, these financial officers are often critical of bankers who have nothing specific to offer – so-called courtesy visits – expect to do business after the first call, or oversell their institution rather than determining what are the corporation's needs. Many financial officers made it clear that prospective bankers can receive a positive welcome only if they have done their homework in advance and are fully competitive in the terms they offer.

When asked to name the criteria used in selecting a new bank relationship, the financial officers cited as the principal factor the offering by a given bank of a new or imaginative solution to a specific problem. Roughly 40 per cent of the respondents cited this factor as their primary consideration, while the ability to accept a specific credit risk ranked as the second most important individual determinant. This emphasis on innovative solutions in a market characterised by little product differentiation places a heavy burden on bankers but it does provide an incentive for the banker to do more than trot out services which are indistinguishable from those of his competitors. The importance of these two criteria taken together also highlights the clients' preference for a one-off specific transaction to initiate a new relationship, rather than an across-the-board approach which might, of course, develop over time.

Recognising that a blend of motives is usually involved in such a decision, another analytical approach is to aggregate the three criteria ranked most highly by individual respondents. The most frequently cited criteria are the two factors already mentioned (imagination and assumption of credit risk) plus the fineness of terms quoted and the speed and responsiveness of the bank's decision-making process, each of which was cited as one of their three top criteria by more than 15, or one-half of the financial officers polled. Other criteria mentioned, in decreasing order of frequency, were the ability of the bank to step up itself for the full amount of a given requirement, personal relationships with the account officer, and flexibility with regard to documentation.

Perhaps the most interesting conclusion to be drawn from the ranking of criteria is the low priority given to the range of services offered by the particular bank, particularly since 'adding to our range of services' is one of the more frequent justifications given by international banks for a particular expansionary move or marketing approach. Fewer than 10 per cent of the respondents thus mentioned size of network and range of services as one of the three most important decision-making criteria. The relative unimportance of this criterion for the larger multinationals can be attributed to their acknowledgement that different banks have different strengths and weaknesses, and that the financial officers prefer to use individual banks for specific one-off purposes which reflect a coincidence of respective skills and requirements – for example, a willingness to accept a particular risk, or an acknowledged skill in moving money from one place to another. Another criterion which surprisingly did not apparently carry more weight with the corporate financial officers was personal relationship with the account officer; only one-quarter of the respondents mentioned this as one of their three principal criteria. Superficially this level of priority would appear inconsistent with the standard corporate criticism that account officers are changed too frequently; on balance, one might conclude that today's corporate treasurers tend to make a more impersonal and objective evaluation of their bank's capabilities and accept, however reluctantly, the frequent rotation of account responsibility. Personal chemistry is always an important factor in this type of relationship, but evidently other considerations of a more objective nature tend to be more important.

By far the most frequently expressed criticism of the business development approach of international banks to corporate solicitation is the lack of preparation and understanding of the latter's business and requirements. This was cited by almost one-half of the respondents as their major criticism of the initial approach by international banks, and by over half as one of the three principal weaknesses of such approach. Three other complaints – the lack of a specific service or product to propose, the inability to commit responsively without time-consuming recourse to home office, and uncompetitive terms – were mentioned as one of their three principal criticisms by roughly one-third of the respondents, while inflexibility and over-legalistic thinking with regard to loan documentation was mentioned as a significant problem by a number of other financial officers. Non-American corporations are particularly sensitive to the frequent practice of American banks of not only insisting on lengthy legal documentation, but also permitting their lawyers to dominate documentary negotiations.

It would thus appear that a significant number of international bankers are perceived not to have done their advance homework before approaching a potential client and therefore find themselves selling a rather undifferentiated product, usually loans or deposit services. A typical quotation is the following from a US corporate treasurer: 'I am somewhat indignant when they start off with the desire and expectation of doing business with this office without doing a nominal amount of homework on our organisation from readily available sources.' And the effort must be a sustained one, to quote a regional treasurer for an oil major: 'Those banks who have successfully made the entry have invariably been willing to undertake a great deal of leg work to find the deal that makes the entry – and then to follow it through. Many banks are not willing to put in this effort.' Another common view was voiced by a corporate treasurer who criticised 'representatives who clearly intend to sell the bank and really have no interest in our group'.

While bankers may be quite convinced of the unique advantages of the services they are selling, corporate treasurers confronted by dozens of such presentations may have a different view. The frustration about international banks' decision-making processes reflects the contrast between the enthusiastic reception of a calling officer interested in establishing a new relationship, and the more considered reaction, often many weeks later, of a senior credit committee which brings other considerations to bear on the proposal.

One specific technique used by international banks to establish an initial relationship is price-cutting, and the responses of the 30 financial officers to a patently below-market quote are quite informative. Over half react positively to such attractive offers of finance or pricing methods, but unless the offering bank has a rational justification for its finer rate – such as a particular knowledge of the credit risk or a specific foreign exchange position of its own – it is almost universally seen to be a loss leader which will be recouped at the client's expense at a later date. Raw price cutting without a rational justification is regarded by a minority of the responding sample as a negative reflection on the professionalism of the bank. Corporate treasurers thus often accept such an underpriced offer as a reflection of the competitive state of the market, but recognise, as the treasurer of a leading UK multinational put it, that 'a bank which quotes terms which are so advantageous to us as to be clearly out of line with the market will win the business but probably not achieve its obvious objective'.

When asked to evaluate existing banking relationships, the respondents cited as their dominant consideration once again the bank's understanding of the customer's business and requirements together with the willingness, which usually stems from such an understanding, of the bank to stick with the customer in difficult circumstances. Almost half of the respondents cited such an understanding as the principal desideratum, while the top criterion mentioned by the second largest number of banks, the fineness of terms quoted, was cited by only 4 of the 30 respondents. If one aggregates the three criteria given the highest priority, understanding of the business (21 responses) and fineness of terms (17 responses) are joined by that of speed and responsiveness of decison-making process (also 17 responses); over one-half of all the respondents thus cited these three considerations as being dominant in their evaluation of existing relationships. It goes without saying that a profound understanding of a client's business can lead not only to fine pricing but also to a quick response time. Other factors mentioned frequently were an imaginative response to a specific problem (12 responses) and the ability of a single bank to meet a given requirement from its own resources (11 responses). Over one-third of the financial officers thus preferred a bank able to avoid the delays and complications often associated with the syndication of a given loan. Only four of the financial officers gave range of services as one of their top three criteria – once again because the large multinationals appear to look to individual banks for their particular strengths and would apparently prefer to pick and choose among a variety of banks.

By relating the criteria applied to new and existing relationships, it would appear that financial officers select new banks on their ability to meet a specific need; once the bank has thus established a relationship, it is evaluated on the basis of its understanding and constancy as well as fineness of pricing and speed of response.

While one can discount some of these reactions as reflecting an understandable preoccupation with the client's own objectives rather than an appreciation of the banker's problems, it is reasonable to conclude that a wide range of international bank calling and account officers do not, in fact, bring with them a reasonable understanding of the potential customer's business and a product or service which is perceived as having some utility to that customer. Business development officers would thus appear to be spending an excessive amount of time in selling their own institution or engaging in social conversation rather than focusing on perceived needs and possible solutions. In many cases the calling officer may not have the necessary expertise to provide the solution desired by the financial officer or, much less, maintain his end of a discussion of possible solutions.

Since this limited survey was carried out, a number of more professional and broadly based studies of this market have been made by specialist research firms. Greenwich Research Associates, for example, on an annual basis surveys multinationals based in North America. In its 1982 study involving 388 interviews with the largest North American firms with overseas affiliates, Greenwich found that the average firm used 23 international banks of which 8 were principal relationships.[2]

These principal relationships were selected primarily on the basis of four factors:

- the existence of a long-term historical relationship;
- an overseas branch network;
- availability of funds when needed;
- high calibre of account officer.

Of declining importance in such a relationship are such factors as:

- competitive loan pricing;
- ability to provide most credit needed.

The single most important factor in the use of a principal bank was given most frequently as:

- competence in global multinational relationships;
- high calibre of account officer;
- overseas branch network.

The reasons for an *improvement* in a bank relationship were found most often to be:

- provision of overseas local currency credit;
- innovation in tailoring loans to needs;
- more competitive loan pricing.

Conversely a *decline* in such a relationship was attributable generally to:

- lack of account officer attention to the company's needs in home and overseas markets;
- uncompetitive loan pricing;
- too much account officer turnover.

In this survey, the importance to multinationals of competent global relationship management was critical. Quality account officers and international advisory services were found to be the decisive elements in developing such a relationship. More specifically, differentiation of international banks is most often based on the characteristics and performance of account officers. Prompt and effective follow-up is clearly the most important characteristic for the account officers to exhibit.

While the two surveys discussed above differ significantly in their time frame, geographic base and breadth, they both point up the challenges faced by international banks in marketing to multinational firms. For example, the latter place a high priority on overseas networks for local currency lending and other products, whereas the banks are finding such networks increasingly expensive to maintain.

More importantly, demands for a global relationship involving a variety of increasingly specialised products place a heavy burden on an account officer who is expected to be well informed on both the client's needs and his own bank's capabilities as well as to mobilise these capabilities in a responsive fashion. Some of the implications of these challenges are discussed in more detail in Chapter 11 on organisational structure.

8 Banking Networks: The Delivery System

A distinguishing feature of the increasing internationalisation of the banking industry in the 1970s and early 1980s has been the proliferation throughout the world of national banks' representative offices, branches, subsidiaries and affiliates. Whereas in previous periods overseas offices were primarily those of 'colonial' banks which provided basic trade-financing services to developing countries, the new breed of such offices post-Second World War has had a variety of objectives. The purpose of this chapter is to describe these objectives, analyse the structure and functioning of the networks and discuss how banks are resolving some of the principal issues which emerge from the growth of overseas networks.

THE OBJECTIVES OF A NETWORK

The principal objectives of a network of offices doing international business – some of which can be located in the parent bank's own national market – can be summarised as follows:

(i) *Euro-currency interbank market dealing:* Tapping the Euro-currency market for wholesale deposits and lending out surplus domestic funds were among the original motivations for establishing the initial elements of an overseas network. German and American banks in particular, faced with regulatory restrictions on lending abroad from domestic sources, have found it necessary to use offshore subsidiaries and branches to take in or lend out their national currencies, while other banks have found it more convenient to open branches in London and other Euro-currency centres than participate in this market primarily through their home office. As the Euro-currency market has broadened and become more sophisticated, major banks are finding it useful to run global deposit and foreign exchange positions which are carried from unit to unit in different time zones throughout the world, so that such an integrated position is truly run on a 24-hour-a-day basis.

A characteristic of the early 1980s has been the mass movement of banks from developing nations to open their initial overseas operating unit for Euro-currency funding purposes. Such banks have found that their credibility as a taker of funds to be on-lent to local clients is enhanced by a branch or agency in a major market such as London or New York.

(ii) *Customer service:* What is essentially a defensive response to the requirements of existing customers has in the past often been the motivation for opening individual branches and representative offices abroad. Such requirements could range from a retail facility for home country tourists or expatriate workers to one which serviced the local requirements of the overseas subsidiary of a domestic corporate customer. In more recent years, however, as the level of competition and costs have increased, other objectives have taken priority.

(iii) *Base for penetrating new markets:* Perhaps the principal such objective in today's market is the penetration of what is for the particular bank a new geographic or functional sector. The combination of physical presence in a given market which facilitates doing business with local corporations and governments, the possibility of tapping sources of local currency funds for on-lending, and the ability to compete directly with local banks which an overseas unit makes possible, have motivated hundreds of banks to set up offices in national markets which appear intrinsically attractive. The potential profitability of a particular functional sector such as merchant banking or leasing has offered similar attractions.

(iv) *Market coverage for existing services:* Another motive of interest primarily to the larger banks is the drive to increase geographic market coverage so as to offer to customers a more comprehensive and efficient service. Such additional links in an international chain may represent a significant competitive advantage over a local or other foreign bank, which cannot service a customer's world-wide requirements as effectively.

(v) *Unit profitability:* Finally the great majority of operating units are expected to provide an incremental profit contribution to the bank in addition to meeting one or more of the above objectives. While many decisions to open new offices are made instinctively by the senior management of a bank, in other cases the decision is preceded by an often elaborate feasibility study which projects incremental costs and revenues. The latter are naturally the more difficult to calculate and often do not represent truly incremental earnings but simply an effective transfer from other areas of the bank which have or could have generated them. In institutions such as American banks, which place a high priority on profitability, new operational units such as branches and subsidiaries are expected to generate satisfactory profits for the bank within a reasonable period of time.

THE CHOICE OF VEHICLE

The choice of individual unit or vehicle and the extent of a network are generally dictated by the bank's strategy as well as the obvious considerations of size and international experience of the bank, availability of human resources, and the nature of the bank's domestic and international business. As these factors evolve along with its international strategy, the bank's attitude towards its network as a whole and the choice of individual units is equally likely to change.

The total absence of an international network presumes a reliance on a bank's own travelling officers, Euro-currency loan participations and overseas correspondent banks as a source of customers, loans and trade-financing opportunities. For relatively small banks without a broad base of experienced management, this solution avoids the expenditure of funds and management time on an overseas network but, correspondingly, does not permit funding access to the Euro-currency market, enable the bank to penetrate new national markets or offer its existing services to potential foreign customers through a locally-based vehicle. A number of smaller national banks have, however, been able to build profitable portfolios of syndicated loan participations and a certain level of trade-related financing without the costly infrastructure of an overseas network.

A representative office – or loan production office, in more recent terminology – represents a relatively low cost effort to achieve the two objectives of customer service and market penetration. Such an office cannot take in or lend funds on its own books and thus permit the parent organisation to participate either in the Euro-currency market or local interbank market, but at least in theory it provides the capability of selling existing services and of generating certain local business which can be booked elsewhere in the network. Banks have found that the annual expenditure of several hundred thousand dollars equivalent necessary to run such an office and the relative facility of closing it down, if business prospects so dictate, make it a very useful preliminary step in exploring a new market. With modern communications technology, however, many banks have found that a loan production office can serve as an effective proxy for a branch in certain markets. Such banks have often converted a deposit-taking branch into a satellite office of a larger branch in the same country or region.

On the other hand, in its business development function the representative office is often hampered by its inability to commit for its own account and therefore its reliance on decision-makers elsewhere in the network. There is also the difficulty of attracting to such a position the successful marketing officer who can have a greater impact on an operating vehicle such as a branch. Finally most banks find it quite difficult to evaluate the performance of an overseas representative whose efforts are usually reflected in other profit centres throughout the bank. Despite these drawbacks, a number of banks who have posted an energetic, experienced and competent officer in such an office have been most pleased with its cost effectiveness in developing profitable business in contrast with the branch alternative.

A branch, on the other hand, can operate as a legal and functional extension of the head office and therefore participate in money markets and develop local business subject to the constraints of local regulations and conditions and the capabilities of its staff. While the annual operating cost is a multiple of that of the representative office because of the additional space and staffing requirements, there is normally no need to put up a significant amount of capital in local currency, and the branch can deal in the market with the full resources of the parent effectively behind it. Perhaps more important in recent years has been the identity and responsiveness provided by such an extension of the parent as banks have found it absolutely necessary in a highly competitive market to establish their own name and ensure that the network is responsive to the strategy established. One useful by-product of establishing a major branch is the banking and management training it can offer to home office personnel as a banking institution in microcosm.

On the other hand, the annual operating expenses of a branch are significantly more than those of a representative office and, in view of the range and integration of dealing, marketing and other functions carried on, are difficult to reduce without impairing the branch's effectiveness. Another problem often encountered is that a substantial portion of the time of the limited number of experienced branch officers is taken up by management rather than revenue-generating preoccupations. A precondition to achieving the specific objectives of a branch is dealing successfully with the host of regulatory, personnel, cultural, linguistic and business problems associated with doing business in a foreign environment, and the handful of senior expatriate and local banking officers in a branch often has limited time left for actually generating revenue after dealing with these concerns. Lastly, the presence of a branch network poses significant problems of delegation of authority and possible duplication of functions with other units of a bank's network. To the extent that the initiative and skills necessary to succeed in branch management exist, there may also be real frustration in organisations where little authority is delegated to the field and each unit has a relatively narrow ambit.

A variant of the branch alternative is the wholly-owned subsidiary which may offer a different range of services than those possible through a branch. Home or host country legislation and other factors may thus require the parent organisation to capitalise the vehicle, which may involve a significant local currency exposure which is not present in the case of a branch. American-owned merchant banks outside the USA, and Luxembourg subsidiaries of German banks are examples of such capitalised vehicles which perform roles not possible in branch offices because of legal and regulatory constraints. In the case of the former, US regulations prohibiting the carrying on of investment banking activities, such as securities underwriting, oblige US banks to perform these operations through overseas subsidiaries exempt from such constraints, while German banks have chosen offshore subsidiaries so as to avoid ratio and other limitations placed on the activities of branches by German regulations.

A final structural option is the joint venture or consortium institution in which the bank joins with one or more partners to establish a capitalised vehicle in an overseas market. While this alternative does not offer the responsiveness and identity desired by many international banks, it may represent the most practical and realistic option for a bank to penetrate a specific functional or geographic market. In recent years, for example, local regulations in a number of highly attractive markets such as Saudi Arabia have effectively required substantial local equity participation as a precondition to entry by a foreign bank. A number of banks have successfully used such a participation as an alternative to a wholly-owned vehicle, particularly during their early international development when they were reluctant to move overseas without the partnership of more experienced institutions who could assist in providing staffing, business development and capital support. In today's market the most successful of these ventures are those which have developed their own management momentum and specialist identity in the market place.

One of the major problems faced by such joint ventures is the evolution over time of individual bank strategies and market conditions which cause adjustment problems often difficult to resolve within the prescribed objectives and fixed shareholdings of the joint company. A consortium which made excellent strategic sense to a group of regional banks in 1973 may, therefore, represent duplication of function in 1982 as the stockholder banks have developed their own Euro-currency business. Another problem which surfaced during the 1974 crisis of confidence is that of ultimate responsibility for funding and depositor liability in the event of serious difficulties. The larger stockholder banks with particular concern for their market reputation often consider that their liability for keeping depositors whole goes well beyond their nominal legal liability as represented by their share of the capital; in such cases they are reluctant to continue as stockholders without the ability to control management performance.

On balance, an interest in a joint venture or consortium thus offers the advantages of partnership with experienced institutions capable of making a contribution to the venture, a relatively low expenditure of capital and management resources in an operating vehicle, and the ability to penetrate markets which local legal or other factors may foreclose to branches and other wholly-owned vehicles. On the other hand, the lack of identity, frequent inability to control management, the possibility of having to bail out other stockholders in the event of a crisis, and the problems which arise when the perceived needs of stockholders change, have significantly reduced the popularity of this alternative since the late 1960s.

THE STRUCTURING OF A NETWORK

The structuring of a network utilising the particular strengths and weaknesses of these types of vehicles involves a careful balancing of a bank's management resources, the potential of given national markets, possible duplication with existing and likely future overseas offices and the nature of a bank's clientele and the products it offers. The initial decisions are usually the easiest: a London or New York branch to provide Euro-currency or dollar funding and develop multinational corporate business in the UK or USA; representative offices or branches in major national markets where existing major customers are located or where a bank's specialist expertise is in great demand; and possibly a branch in another major regional market such as Asia to provide funding and incremental business in that region.

As the network expands, however, the decisions become more difficult. First, existing management resources become stretched; the variety of credit, personnel, cultural, marketing and management skills required to successfully manage an overseas unit are found in a limited number of individuals whose services may be better utilised in home office. A bank struggling to develop international corporate lending, marketing and other skills can often not spare such scarce talent to open up a far-off office.

Another people-related problem is the motivation and eventual reabsorption of experienced overseas officers elsewhere in the network. An energetic and competent overseas officer, particularly during periods when international business is regarded by the bank as relatively unattractive, can become quite frustrated if he perceives interesting business opportunities in his local market which are consistently rejected by his superiors in home office. When the time comes for eventual transfer to headquarters, he may regret the loss of the relative degree of authority and responsibility associated with such a transfer to the extent of leaving the bank in order to remain in the market he has come to know.

The understandable practice of using major overseas offices such as London branches as a training ground for high potential senior managers poses additional problems. While a domestically trained or relatively inexperienced international banker obtains a good deal of useful experience through a two or three-year tour in such an office, what usually suffers is the morale of local staff denied promotional opportunities, as well as customers who, every few years, must deal with a new account officer who is transferred at just about the time he becomes useful to them.

A second problem area relates to the cost and complexity of the administrative apparatus necessary to support a large network of overseas offices. Such an apparatus seems to grow more rapidly than the actual network in terms of expense and claims on management time. As the number of overseas employees rises, a sophisticated personnel infrastructure dealing with a host of compensation, regulatory, transfer, accommodation, tax and other problems becomes necessary. Transfer of officers to and from an offshore location comes to involve a host of decisions as to housing, allowances, compensation, job content and other factors which must be resolved to the individual's reasonable satisfaction to retain his motivation and commitment. Management information systems co-ordinating and controlling the network's dealing and lending functions become more expensive and complex. Procedures must be established, for example, to allocate among different overseas units a global credit limit for individual customers and banks. More management time must be spent in planning, co-ordination and marketing meetings for overseas staff to establish and implement strategic programmes. Once established, this plethora of staff functions is difficult to reduce and tends to grow steadily in cost and complexity.

Another cost-related problem is the general impact of rising costs on the economics of an overseas network. In addition to the growth in a non-revenue generating but costly administrative hierachy described above, international banks have suffered from the general inflation of unit costs of the late 1970s and early 1980s. Moreover, cost pressures have been intensified by the need to bid competitively for scarce resources. Whether it be renting modern office space in a central location, recruiting a successful foreign exchange dealer or hiring a skilled energy specialist, international banks find themselves bidding up the price of these limited resources.

The net impact of these cost-related factors has been to transform the economics of delivering products through an overseas network. Table 8.1 summarises the results of a survey of a sample of London-based international banks which compares the level of operating expenses in 1973 and 1980. The 150 per cent increase in such expenses over this seven-year period would, in many if not most cases, more than offset the normal revenue growth from higher interest and fee income. The resulting issue of network cost effectiveness is discussed later in this chapter.

From a business development and marketing point of view, an expanded network creates real pressures on management to restructure the bank's organisation and decision-making functions to respond more effectively to customer requirements and the natural desire of overseas officers to operate with a greater

TABLE 8.1   Increase in Annual Operating Expenses of Typical London-based Branch or Euro-bank

		(In $ thousands)		
		1973	1980	% Increase
Small bank[a]				
Personnel expenses		250	700	180
Other operating expenses[c]		350	800	129
	TOTAL	600	1500	150
Medium-sized bank[b]				
Personnel expenses		350	900	157
Other operating expenses[c]		450	1100	144
	TOTAL	800	2000	150

[a] Small bank defined as one with approximately 20 in staff capable of managing total assets of $100–250 million.
[b] Medium-sized bank has staff of about 35 which handles assets in the region of $500 million.
[c] Excludes provision for loan losses and taxes on income.

Source: Interviews of 10 bank sample conducted in 1973 and 1980 by the author.

degree of autonomy. In response to these pressures, the major American banks have either significantly increased the level of authority delegated to the field or reorganised in the direction of the geographic/functional matrix-structures described in Chapter 11. While such restructuring is intellectually satisfying and often quite effective in the marketplace, the disruption caused by such an organisational change and the inevitable increase in time spent on internal co-ordination have gone some way to offset the obvious advantage of a large overseas network.

Perhaps a more serious problem is simply the level of competition in local markets which has built up over time through the arrival of new foreign banks and their marketing techniques as well as the responses of local institutions. While the first American branches in a market such as the UK or Germany thus profited considerably from relatively unprospected opportunities in a hitherto highly structured market, those banks opening up in these markets since the late 1960s have had a more difficult row to hoe.

Finally the management of a large and growing network inevitably involves the more precise definition of roles of individual units and attempts to reconcile effective management control with the need to motivate overseas management and compete effectively in the marketplace. In a large and far-flung network, the response of many American and other banks has been to establish regional headquarters with line and/or staff relationships to overseas units in that region. In its ultimate extreme, such a regional headquarters assumes most of the credit and other decision-making authority of home office, whose role is limited to the establishing of world-wide policy guidelines, planning and control of performance. In more limited versions, a large branch or regional office can provide staff support to local units in sectors such as personnel, credit, tax, marketing and accounting.

The success of regional delegation has been a function of the willingness of senior management in home office to truly delegate such line and staff functions, the real and perceived influence and competence of officers at various levels in the field and, of course, the financial and marketing results achieved. It goes without saying that a major loss or other disaster stemming from delegated authority is not conducive to continuation of such delegation. True delegation of line authority, particularly in the lending function, requires a degree of self denial and abstinence on the part of home office staff which, in many cases of active and experienced individuals, is difficult to achieve. Without such real delegation and the implicit home office support that goes with it, however, a regional office may be counter-productive in that it becomes an additional – and often expensive – link in an already long administrative chain, which is increasingly circumvented by officers in the field who naturally seek out the ultimate source of authority. On the other hand, where real delegation of authority in line or staff matters exists and where overseas officers effectively utilise their increased flexibility, the impact on morale, profits and customer satisfaction has been impressive.

SPECIFIC MANAGEMENT RESPONSES

Management interviews in connection with the 1978 questionnaire produced some interesting views with regard to networks and their likely future development. While such results inevitably reflect conditions and views as of mid-1978, they do have some validity in a longer term context. Of the 38 banks which characterised their present networks, roughly equal numbers fell into three arbitrarily defined categories as follows:

(i) offices/branches which do *extensive local as well as international* business in a large number of national markets abroad;

(ii) offices/branches in most or all of the world's *leading financial centres* which primarily carry on *international* business; and

(iii) offices/branches only in a *limited* number of offshore centres so as to permit home office *access* to the international market.

In addition, two of the banks fell into the final category:

(iv) no offshore offices beyond a *limited* number of *representatives* who do not do business directly.

While these categorisations are admittedly arbitrary, they do correspond roughly to the articulated expansion strategies of a number of banks. The institutions were then asked to determine whether their network was:

(a) largely in place (given current market conditions);
(b) some expansion was likely to occur; or
(c) a major network increase was in prospect.

Of the 38 banks responding, 23, or roughly 60 per cent, indicated that their networks were largely in place (a), while another third foresaw some expansion (b). There was no significant differentiation between the sample of American/Canadian banks and the other institutions in terms of likely expansion prospects. Of equal interest is the indication that banks with less developed networks are likely, despite the pressures on profitability which existed in mid-1978, to continue to expand their overseas operations. Of the 12 banks in category (i) – the largest and most sophisticated networks – only one-third predicted any marked level of further expansion (categories b and c), while of the 13 institutions in category (iii) – a limited number of units to provide market access – roughly two-thirds foresaw such a likely increase.

These admittedly fragmentary results would appear to support external evidence indicating that, almost regardless of nationality and current market conditions, banks developing their international networks follow an almost predictable pattern within an overall strategic plan. The need for, say, a Tokyo branch or a New York office is regarded as a strategic requirement which hopefully can be justified financially under current market conditions. While a relatively mature bank may thus be agonising over whether to close an office in a given market because of a poor profit outlook, a less advanced competitor may be about to open one across the street.

THE PROBLEM OF COST EFFECTIVENESS

Another set of questions revealed some interesting insights into the role played by quantifiable results in the decisions to open, operate and possibly close an overseas office. While virtually all banks interviewed analyse the potential profitability of a proposed overseas operating unit such as a branch or affiliate, a sharp division of attitude is shown when it is assumed, for purposes of argument, that an existing operating unit is demonstrably unlikely to produce, directly or indirectly, satisfactory quantifiable results for the bank as a whole. Faced with what is seen to be a source of future overall losses over an extended period of time, roughly half of the US and Canadian banks interviewed would be prepared to close down a branch or other operating unit despite the possible damage of such a closure to its reputation and the difficulty of re-entering that national market at a future point in time. None of the non-North American institutions, however, would be prepared to take such an action, arguing that a longer-term and non-financial view must be taken of the attractiveness of the given market, government and customer relationships and the possible damage to a bank's image.

A different attitude is often shown towards representative offices which are seen to be less visible overseas outposts with less easily quantifiable outputs. American and other banks alike often regard these less expensive units as a necessary customer and marketing service whose results do not have to be quantified. On the other hand, should market conditions change or perceived results prove disappointing, a much larger proportion of banks is prepared to close down a representative office. A similar pragmatic approach is taken towards minority interests in consortium banks; a fairly large proportion of banks around the world has no hesitation about selling out of a consortium – if possible – if given profit and other objectives are not achieved.

Such a pragmatic viewpoint on the part of American banks in particular reflects not only their greater concern with overall, long term profitability, but also the rising cost level associated with maintenance of an overseas network. The general vulnerability of a personnel-intensive service operation has been discussed above. As a bank moves along its international life cycle to the point at which profitability drives its strategic thinking, the vision of a globe dotted with one's offices is replaced by the concern over the network's profit contribution. Whereas a branch in the 1960s could produce an attractive profit from a given level of risk assets and fees, the doubling and tripling of operating expenses since then has called into question the economics of such a delivery system.

Profit-conscious institutions have, therefore, become increasingly concerned with the cost-effectiveness of a given overseas network.

During the early 1980s a number of US and other banks have undergone a thorough review of their networks in connection with a reassessment of their competitive strategy. To quote one such banker, 'we have sculpted the organisation'[1]. Such a review has generally pointed up the limited profit prospects for foreign-owned units in open, sophisticated markets such as Japan, the USA and Western Europe where local competition has become a more effective force. Another argument for network reduction or consolidation is the development of modern data-processing and communication technology which permits direct customer interface with remote locations for foreign exchange trading, the deposit and movement of funds and other transactions which traditionally have taken place on the spot in a local operating unit.

On the other hand, multinational client surveys such as those described in Chapter 7 have pointed up the need for comprehensive services provided by an extensive overseas network as well as the virtues of local expertise and direct customer contact in the field.

The response to this dilemma of banks with significant networks has been one of rationalisation rather than major surgery. Every effort has been made to structure and improve a major bank's ability to deliver wholesale banking products to multinational clients. Representative offices in secondary markets have been closed or transformed, through a change of personnel and nomenclature, into a loan production office whose objectives are geared to the generation of incremental revenues rather than the passive servicing of existing relationships. Branches or other operating units in low priority markets have been closed or reduced to such a loan production office; in Germany, for instance, a US bank might close a Munich or Hamburg branch but retain a Frankfurt presence.

Within a given unit, a major restructuring might take place. Low profit or low priority functions such as a retail banking capability, a letter of credit department or a dealing function might be closed or consolidated with a larger facility in an adjacent market. A move to lower cost premises outside the financial district could take place. Rather than suffer the possible business and prestige loss from actually closing an operating unit, a bank might restructure it into a highly specialised role such as a link in a cash management, money dealing or investment management network.

For even the most profit-conscious banks, however, the non-financial considerations involved in closing overseas offices in major market centres such as London often swing the decision. A number of international heads of regional banks interviewed have recommended such closure to senior management which has not concurred because of considerations relating to personal and corporate prestige, and the decision to take a longer-term view in spite of the acknowledged lack of utility of the office in the bank's present international posture. In a number of cases, the difficulty of quantifying a unit's overall contribution and the commitment of key individuals in an organisation reinforce the natural reluctance to be seen to be retrenching. On the other hand, a significant number of American banks feel that, properly explained to the outside world in terms of the constructive need to divert resources elsewhere in the network, the announcement of closing an office can have a net positive impact on a bank's market standing.

European and Japanese banks, however, are quick to criticise what can be regarded as a short-sighted decision, and they quote the number of instances when US and other banks have pulled out of markets under difficult conditions and thereby significantly impaired their ability to re-enter when the market became more attractive. Most major continental European banks went so far in the interviews as to state that they would only close an operating unit overseas if literally forced to by external conditions such as nationalisation or civil conflict. The actual behaviour of US banks to date reflects this thinking as it relates to units in major international markets such as London and national markets such as Paris. Only a handful of branches in these centres had been closed by 1982 despite highly unattractive profit prospects.

ATTITUDES TOWARDS CONSORTIA

Finally responses to the questionnaire with regard to attitudes toward joint ventures and consortium institutions confirmed evidence during the late 1970s and early 1980s of a marked swing of interest away from such participations. Of the 38 banks responding, only seven (18 per cent) considered that a joint venture or consortium participation was a useful option which should play a role in their overseas stategy. The remaining responses varied from an absolute prohibition on such participations to the statement that an uphill fight would be necessary to sell such a venture within the bank. Most banks acknowledged that local regulations and market conditions might necessitate the use of a specific joint venture or consortium approach, but the distinct preference among at least four-fifths of the banks was to find a solution which at least permitted them to retain overall management control, if not 100 per cent ownership, of a venture whose role was carefully defined, with partners who were certain to be compatible and make a significant contribution.

The predominantly negative attitudes towards less than 100 per cent ownership of a vehicle stem not only from the general factors discussed previously in this chapter – an evolution of strategy, the greater emphasis on network identity and responsiveness, etc. – but also direct experience in individual consortia and joint ventures. While some of these institutions have made notable progress in profit generation and market impact, the majority have shown a relatively unimpressive return on capital and assets. More to the point, in some cases parent banks have suffered actual losses and/or damage to their image from support provided to affiliates requiring funding or transfer of bad loans to remain viable.

Many bankers admit, however, that attitudes to joint ventures ebb and flow, and that such emotion in mid-1978 was particularly negative. What many bankers tend to forget is the utility of such a participation to less mature institutions and, in fact, to their own at a given point in the past. It is easy to forget that a relative newcomer to the international scene may very justifiably select a joint venture or minority participation as an alternative to a branch or representative office as an initial step into the Euro-currency market.

The problems tend to arise over time as individual strategies and market conditions evolve and it becomes institutionally difficult to restructure or otherwise modify an entity which has also generated its own personality and momentum. It is also evident that, with perfect hindsight, the long-term compatibility of partners and strategy of the joint venture vehicle was, in many cases, not sufficiently thought out. The fact remains, however, that roughly one-fifth of the banks interviewed profess themselves essentially pleased with their existing consortium and joint venture interests and would positively consider new ones.

9 The Treasury Function

Asset and liability management – often called treasury management – is the integrated management of such key asset and liability variables as maturity, yield, quality and liquidity to achieve the appropriate balance of profitability and liquidity. The purpose of this chapter is to describe how international banks have approached this task and the issues which they confront in treasury management.

EVOLUTION OF INTERNATIONAL ASSET/LIABILITY MANAGEMENT

The evolution of integrated international balance sheet management originates with the Euro-currency interbank foreign exchange and deposit markets based in London in the early 1960s. As mentioned previously, an international bank's initial dealing activities usually commence with meeting customer foreign exchange requirements and funding domestic or international loans. From such essentially matched transactions, banks began to take interest and exchange rate exposures by anticipating changes in these rates, and in many cases significant profits were earned from these positions. In organisations such as US banks with a relatively independent international funding operation, this became a net supplier or taker of funds from the domestic side of the bank, and appropriate 'pool' rates were applied to this net flow. In addition to these funding operations, domestic banks began in the 1960s to price their loans to overseas customers on a floating rate or LIBOR basis, which necessitated bidding for such floating rate deposits in the interbank market.

The unique character of Euro-currency funding – based primarily on purchased funds priced in relation to assets of equivalent roll-over maturity – introduced new elements into traditional bank asset and liability management. Historically, in a typical domestic environment of relatively cheap demand deposits, low interest rate volatility and controlled loan growth, banks used either intuitive techniques or ones which allocated specific liabilities to various asset categories so as to ensure the desired degree of liquidity and interest rate exposure.

With the ability to expand their asset base simply by bidding for interbank deposits which could match equivalent asset maturities with a contractual profit margin, banks operating in the Euro-markets developed new asset/liability management techniques. Much greater reliance was placed on bidding for new deposits to meet liquidity needs rather than selling liquid assets: the 'liability' method thus progressively replaced the 'stock' or 'asset allocation' strategy.

ROLES OF THE TREASURY FUNCTION

As the international bank's treasury function evolved, three distinct roles of the senior treasury or asset/liability manager have become clear:

- Finance manager or controller
- Profit centre manager
- Product manager

FINANCE MANAGER

This role involves controlling the various risks inherent in any international treasury function:

- liquidity
- interest rate exposure
- foreign exchange exposure
- counterpart credit.

(i) *Liquidity:* By their nature, banks are engaged in the business of maturity transformation, that is, converting relatively short-term deposits into comparatively longer-term loans and other assets. While in their domestic lending business a major portion of assets in the form of overdrafts and advances are at least nominally of short-term maturity, in the Euro-currency market the contractual maturity of loans extends to ten years or more with the result that the average life of a typical Euro-currency loan portfolio is several years or longer, but is being funded to a preponderant extent by wholesale money market deposits with an average maturity of several months.

The consequent vulnerability of international banks to the inability to renew these deposits was magnified by the practice of mismatching, or short funding, rollover deposit maturities to obtain the profit from funding at a lower cost than the stated rate on the asset financed. While this practice might involve increasing the average maturity of deposits if the dealer predicted an increase in interest rates, more often it meant taking shorter-term deposits in view of the upward-sloping yield curve for longer maturities which normally exists in the major Euro-currency markets.

While unable to eliminate the liquidity threat, international banks have taken a variety of steps to minimise liquidity risk. The most obvious is to present to major depositors – principally other banks – an image of total conservatism and to maintain close personal relationships with such bank and non-bank depositors. Depositor confidence is a vital element in any banking operation, but the unusual dependence of international banks on money market funds and the absence of an obvious international lender of last resort, mean that exceptional measures must be taken to retain the confidence of major depositors. Relatively new entrants to the Euro-currency market, regardless of size or position in their domestic market, thus build up their Euro-currency business gradually as lines are made available to them by established banks. Such efforts received new impetus following the Herstatt crisis of confidence in 1974 when funds tended to flow to the largest, best known and presumably safest institutions at the expense of the smaller, newer and other banks which were perceived as carrying a higher level of depositor risk.

A second policy has been to attempt to quantify a bank's ability to tap the international market, and in this context to establish limits on the extent to which assets are mismatched for given periods of time on a rollover basis. Efforts are also made to avoid over-dependence on one or a group of depositors and to build up the level of customer-related deposits which are presumed to be less volatile because of the closer relationship with the bank. Often elaborate mismatch or gap limits thus limit the extent to which a bank must have recourse to the interbank market for a given period to fund such maturity gaps. A cash flow ladder by time period (daily, weekly or monthly) is constructed to reflect all cash transactions (loan repayments, deposit maturities, foreign exchange purchases and sales, and so on), and arbitrary limits on net positions are established by time period or on a cumulative basis.

Thirdly, international banks have established liquidity reserves in the form of negotiable instruments and other assets which can be mobilised in the event of difficulties in renewing deposits. In some cases, standby facilities from friendly or related institutions are utilised to supplement these reserves. Finally, international banks have been able to issue negotiable dollar-denominated certificates of deposit and floating rate notes with a contractual maturity approaching or equivalent to that of their loan portfolio. While such issues can only represent a fraction of the total loan book, they do reduce the liquidity exposure significantly, and the banking authorities of many countries outside the USA have encouraged their national institutions to undertake such issues. Given the extent of dependence of most international banks on money market funds, however, it is recognised that such measures in the face of a total inability to renew deposits can provide liquidity only for a limited period of time, following which any necessary support must be obtained from central bank or other outside sources.

One possible solution to liquidity problems which is adopted only *in extremis* is the paying of a premium over the appropriate market interest rate to obtain funds. While there can be some disagreement as to the appropriate rate for any given bank at a particular time, the market is extraordinarily sensitive to banks perceived to be paying 'over the odds' for funds, a phenomenon which, particularly in periods of high market tension as in 1974 and 1982, is interpreted to imply that the particular institution is in difficulty. Such self-fulfilling prophecies probably did occur in the post-Herstatt tension, and banks – particularly the smaller and newer institutions – have gone to great lengths to avoid what they regard as tarnishing their name through overbidding for funds.

These issues of liquidity risk from deposit mis-matching in the Euro-currency market are even more difficult to resolve in the case of those banks operating abroad in national money markets, which do not have the breadth of such Euro-currencies as the Euro-dollar, Euro-Deutschmark and Euro-Swiss Franc. As overseas banks have been attracted to the profit potential of lending in local currency to customers in such countries as France, Germany and Spain, they are faced at least initially with almost total dependence for deposits on a local interbank market often dominated by a handful of large national banks who are not only their natural competitors, but who also use this market largely as a safety valve for excess funds. This safety valve can obviously be turned off when money is tight. Such markets are often comparatively new and thus offer relatively short maturities and are capable of violent movements as a result of change in local monetary conditions. In such instances, international banks generally resort to back-up support lines from local institutions as well as absolute controls on exposure to these markets.

A related issue is the problem of access to dollars for non-dollar based banks. The US dollar, as the world's principal reserve currency, as well as the natural choice of the American banks which have played the dominant role in the Euro-currency market, remains the currency of denomination of most Euro-currency loans. The reliance on the Euro-currency inter-bank market to fund a large portfolio of dollar-denominated loans has seriously inhibited many non-dollar-based banks from expanding their international operations. Over time, however, such banks have been able to establish direct US operations through branching and acquisition, and have also gained greater confidence in their ability as a prominent international institution to create Euro-dollars even in time of crisis. The ability of virtually all international banks to attract dollars, even in the very serious psychological crisis of the Herstatt period, has thus quietened some of these concerns.

(ii) *Interest rate exposure:* while the concept of pricing loans over the cost of matching deposits theoretically eliminates an international bank's exposure to adverse interest rate movements, in practice deliberate mismatch positions are taken in the context of the treasury's role as a profit centre. In addition, there may be occasions when it is physically impossible because of market conditions for an individual bank to obtain a matching deposit at the time the loan is priced.

The subject of deliberate mismatching of deposit maturities, like that of foreign exchange positions, is one of great sensitivity to international bankers. Many bankers believe that admitting to such a policy conflicts with their desire to project an image of total conservatism – hence the frequency of claims that such a phenomenon does not exist in one's own bank.

Whether acknowledged or not, most banks consciously or unconsciously assume some degree of interest rate risk in their international operations. The more sophisticated institutions concentrate their efforts on quantifying this exposure, estimating the possible loss or gain from a given interest rate movement, evaluating the likelihood of such movements, and placing limits on exposure so as not to suffer undue loss.

As banks become more highly motivated by the goal of profit maximisation, greater pressure is placed on the international dealing function to obtain the funding profit which is associated with an upward sloping or normal yield curve. The Euro-dollar yield curve has more often than not permitted banks, for example, to fund a six-month roll-over loan with overnight or one month borrowing at a profit, although periodically losses have been incurred from an upward movement of the yield curve or a reverse, or downward sloping curve.

To limit such losses, international banks establish absolute and relative limits on the gaps in their cash flow ladder for individual currencies. The average cost and yield of existing assets and liabilities for each maturity are calculated and the resulting net position, if any, is 'marked to market' by determining the profit or loss if covered at current or projected future interest rates. Some banks have the computerised capability of analysing 'what if' possibilities of interest rate movements and the consequent impact on profit and loss. Table 9.1 shows a sample interest sensitivity report used by a major US bank.

Sources and uses of funds are shown on a monthly basis for repricing out to one year with a separate category for assets and liabilities without a fixed maturity. Actual rates received and paid on these funds are shown together with the net matched and unmatched position by maturity period, the net margin (or loss) locked in, and the rate which must be obtained on the unmatched portion to break even. The final column shows the cumulative mismatched position together with current market rates which can be compared with the breakeven rates to determine potential profit or loss at current interest rates.

TABLE 9.1 Interest Sensitivity Report by Maturity Period

Sample Interest Rate
Sensitivity Analysis (in $MM) for US Dollar Position

Repriced during following month	Total Uses		Total Sources[a]		Matched		Unmatched		Cumulative	Unmatched Rate
	Amount	Rate	Amount	Rate	Amount	Rate	Amount	Rate	Amount	
No fixed maturity[b]	592	5.29	1629	9.40	592	(4.11)	1037	9.40	1002	15.09
Current month	2148	15.24	2758	14.53	2148	0.71	610	14.53	1612	15.06
Month 2	2026	15.48	2145	14.83	2026	0.65	119	14.83	1731	14.96
Month 3	2819	15.10	2546	14.96	2819	0.14	(273)	15.10	1458	14.89
Month 4	1343	15.27	995	14.83	1343	0.44	(348)	15.27	1110	14.77
Month 5	1120	14.59	628	14.96	1120	(0.37)	(492)	14.59	618	14.84
Month 6	1262	15.28	461	14.54	1262	0.74	(801)	15.28	(183)	15.01
Month 7	587	15.73	383	14.99	587	0.74	(204)	15.73	(387)	15.01
Month 8	86	15.39	134	15.31	86	0.08	48	15.31	(339)	14.98
Month 9	50	15.59	291	15.17	50	0.42	241	15.17	(98)	14.94
Month 10	42	13.16	260	15.42	42	(2.08)	218	15.24	120	13.80
Month 11	146	14.78	125	14.49	146	(0.29)	(21)	14.78	99	13.64
Month 12	14	14.98	113	15.28	14	(0.30)	99	15.28	198	13.62
Month 13	29	15.72	65	15.50	29	0.22	36	15.50	234	13.55
1–2 years	333	14.20	306	15.10	333	(0.90)	(27)	14.20	207	13.15
2–3 years	164	14.02	127	15.63	164	(1.61)	(37)	4,02	170	12.77
3 years +	372	12.77	202	13.77	372	(1.00)	(170)	12.77	—	—
Total	13,133	14.65	13,168	14.14	13,133	0.51	35	14.14	35	14.14

Notes: [a] includes equity.
[b] includes demand deposits, call loans, non-interest bearing assets, capital, non-interest bearing liabilities.
[c] net of $35mm in net liabilities.

(iii) *Foreign exchange exposure:* some degree of exposure in the form of a time mismatch is inevitable even in passively responding to client requirements unless the bank is simply playing a brokerage, rather than a dealing, function. The rapid and often violent movement of exchange rates and the difficulty of off-loading a position immediately on the market thus create such mismatches even in the most conservative dealing strategies.

Most banks take a more aggressive stance by actively anticipating foreign exchange and interest rate changes in their spot and forward exchange positions. The movement away from central-bank-defended fixed parities in the early 1970s significantly increased the level of uncertainty in a market which heretofore had often been able to profit from a one-way option. Moreover, the natural human instinct of dealers to take advantage of what they considered profit opportunities led to the taking of positions in spot and forward exchange which often had little or nothing to do with customers' or the bank's own requirements. While limits and controls on foreign exchange exposure existed from the outset in most international banks, they were often ignored or circumvented – sometimes with the concurrence of managements which placed an extraordinary amount of confidence in their dealer's ability to turn a profit – until a series of various well-publicised losses in 1974 from unauthorised dealing and overtrading so shocked the market that elaborate control mechanisms were established and enforced throughout the international banking sector.

In most banks, foreign exchange exposure controls are applied by individual currency (against the 'home' currency) and in aggregate. Open positions – the sum of all assets (including forward contracts) in a given currency less all liabilities – are limited, usually to a given fraction of the bank's stockholder funds. Forward exposure by currency, both for individual future period gaps and cumulative (adding plusses and minuses for subsequent periods) positions, are also limited, usually to an amount related to stockholder funds.

While many banks do limit their foreign exchange activity to customer-related transactions and the creation of deposits through swaps, a number of institutions express such a policy publicly to enhance their image as a conservative bank. In reality, however, the great bulk of exchange activity among banks has a purely speculative rather than client base. A 1980 study of the Federal Reserve Bank of New York indicated that, assuming each customer order requires between four and six transactions to effect cover, one half of the increase in turnover in the New York market between 1977 and 1980 was accounted for by pure interbank dealing. In the spot market alone, which represented two-thirds of total activity, interbank deals in 1980 exceeded customer deals by a factor of 20.[1]

The substantial increase in purely speculative interbank activity has resulted in a significant increment in the level of risk associated with an active foreign exchange dealing function. Whether a bank's dealing strategy involves taking short-term intra-day positions or a longer-term view, it is essentially pitting its judgement against a market which is becoming increasingly competitive and sophisticated.

(iv) *counterpart credit:* while individual credit judgements are generally the responsibility of other functions in the bank, the treasurer's role is to ensure that the risks of a failure of a counterpart to meet its commitments are controlled in a systematic fashion.

The most obvious need for controls is on deposit exposure to other banks in the interbank market, where counterpart failure can mean loss of the entire deposit amount. Such limits take into consideration the counterpart's net worth and perceived credit quality, the duration of exposure, the bank's own level of dealing activity, and other business relationships with the counterpart. Foreign exchange lines, where counterpart failure requires covering in the market at a potential gain or loss, are generally set at a multiple of the deposit line.

A final dimension of counterpart credit is settlement exposure, or the total amount due from a counterpart on a given day. Such limits became prevalent following the substantial losses incurred in 1974 by banks which had delivered Deutschmarks to Bankhaus Herstatt but did not receive the corresponding dollar amount of the foreign exchange transaction because of the bank's closure during the settlement day.

In managing these various risks, the finance manager or treasurer is often assisted by a group variously termed the Asset and Liability or Alco Committee on which may sit senior lending officers, economists and treasury personnel. Such a group may function to co-ordinate views on treasury-related issues as well as exchange ideas on interest and exchange rate prospects. While this type of committee often serves as a useful communications vehicle, most banks find that action responsibility must be delegated to a single individual, generally the treasurer or finance manager.

PROFIT CENTRE MANAGER

The role of the treasury function as a profit centre naturally becomes more critical as an international bank's strategy is driven increasingly by the need to maximise profits. Such profits can be derived from taking a successful long-term view on interest or exchange rates to produce a running profit, by trading deposits or exchange to earn a short-term profit, by reducing the cost of funding through successful bidding for relatively inexpensive deposits, or reducing the cost of liquidity.

A variety of factors inhibit the setting of specific profit targets for the treasury function. The high correlation of risk and reward, the understandable concern that over-ambitious targets might encourage over-aggressive dealing, the difficulty of predicting market conditions conducive to profitable dealing – all militate against making the type of profit forecasts which are provided by other functions in a bank. Many international banks resort to rules of thumb, such as a yield of $\frac{1}{4}-\frac{1}{2}$ per cent under LIBOR as a profit target for the combined matched and mismatched funding profit obtained from the interbank market.

Others take into consideration historical profit levels and an *ex-post* evaluation of trading opportunities to determine whether the dealing function took adequate advantage of such favourable developments as a sharp drop in interest rates or a high level of foreign exchange activity. Single point profit targets are less frequent than a range which takes into consideration the level of trading opportunities.

A bank with global treasury reach in the form of a significant corporate client base, dealing functions in a variety of local markets and the ability to manage its position on a 24-hour basis in different markets clearly has the potential to earn greater treasury profits than one without these advantages. In major dealings markets such as London, treasury profits for a global bank by the early 1980s had come to represent a substantial portion of total earnings in that market.

PRODUCT MANAGER

The treasury function also provides products both internally to the bank and externally to its clients. Internally its views on interest and exchange rate prospects as well as market conditions assist management in setting policy regarding risk positions, liquidity and capital. The lending function is assisted by competitive and flexible funding.

Externally the treasury function may be responsible for the substantive input for a variety of fee-earning, advisory products. Foreign exchange and interest rate advice is one of the non-credit products most highly valued by multinational clients. Discretionary advice on managing a portfolio of liquid, fixed rate investments is another significant product sold to a variety of government and private sector clients.

ISSUES IN ASSET/LIABILITY MANAGEMENT

As an international bank becomes increasingly reliant on profits from its treasury function, it confronts the issue of dependence on highly volatile earnings with a high risk coefficient.

Some banks are fortunate to have a dealing team which can produce reasonably consistent, growing profit levels without taking substantial risk positions, but the performance volatility of even the best dealing teams is shown by the sharp fluctuations in foreign exchange earnings reported by the major US banks. By the same token, misjudgements of interest rate movement – usually hidden in overall data on net interest income – have been made by some of the most sophisticated and experienced national banks.

Another issue relating to dealing operations is the growing complexity and possible duplication which arises as an international bank expands its overseas network of branches and affiliates, each of which may have a separate dealing function. While each operating unit of the network may have its own loan portfolio to fund and a certain amount of local currency business to transact, the great bulk of the business of the dealing room of the typical overseas branch is in exchange and deposit trading in the major Euro-currencies. From a purely intellectual standpoint it should be possible to restrict the size and nature of each unit's money and exchange book to meeting the specific funding and other operations of that particular unit. However, in the real world it is difficult to attract and motivate good dealers whose sole role, for example, might be to fund customer and branch loan requirements on a purely matched basis, while global mismatch positions are taken elsewhere in the bank. In many cases such units can justify taking positions locally on the basis of their particular skills, local market conditions and the particular advantage of their time zone. On balance, however, most banks with extensive Euro-currency dealing operations have moved towards a structure whereby the principal deposit and foreign exchange exposures are taken in one or a limited number of financial centres often on the basis of shifting their position from one time zone to another to maximise profit opportunities and improve co-ordination. Other dealing units are then given quite restricted limits, presumably related primarily to local requirements. This structure does not prevent, however, dealers' natural competitive instincts from attempting to maximise local unit profitability through dealing often in competition or at variance with other units of their bank.

This issue of centralisation vs. decentralisation of the treasury function is increasingly being resolved by concern over risk control in favour of a centralised structure. In the early 1980s, as banks with multiple dealing operations became concerned over the global risk position resulting from the efforts of individual units, they have tended to limit the dealing flexibility of such units by imposing global limits established by senior treasury officers in the head office.

A related organisational issue for many banks is the relationship between, on the one hand, Euro-currency and other international money dealing and, on the other, purely domestic money market operations. For continental European banks organised along functional lines which have a fully integrated treasury function incorporating both domestic and international operations, this is not a problem. For US and other institutions organised primarily on a territorial basis, however, there are growing pressures to integrate at least the funding operations on a world-wide basis to take maximum advantage of arbitrage possibilities between the domestic currency and its Euro-equivalent, and minimise duplication of effort. The continuing existence of a higher rate of interest on equivalent maturity

Euro-dollars over domestic US dollar deposits and CDs, is one example of the profit opportunities available to US and other banks who can borrow funds in the USA and lend them on a matched basis in London or other countries. At the personnel level, the decision by many US banks to transfer key senior Euro-currency dealers to home office not only increased the level of dealing skills there, but also tended to decrease the level of intrabank competition and duplication of effort among their various dealing rooms throughout the world. North American banks in particular have moved to a functional treasury structure in which dealing personnel in overseas offices report to treasury management in home office rather than geographic officers such as branch managers.

Over time, a number of US and other institutions have thus brought an increasing portion of their global balance sheet under unified management. Often supervised by an assets/liabilities management committee, such a management group makes bank-wide decisions as to level and location of mismatch, foreign exchange positions, arbitrage policy, choice and maturity of liabilities (such as Federal Funds, Certificates of Deposit and time deposits) for funding purposes, level and composition of liquidity, extent and location of fixed rate lending, and other judgements on the basis of common assumptions of interest and exchange rate movements. Whether this function remains within the international area of a bank is largely a matter of the relative skills and influence of the key individuals involved, as well as the relative importance of international funding to the bank. In the process of thus breaking down the barriers between international and domestic market operations, banks have often discovered significant new profit opportunities through the integrated management of the bulk of their assets and liabilities. Not only are arbitrage operations facilitated and new opportunities exploited through better human communications, but also senior management has been able to make more efficient use of its overall balance sheet because of the greater degree of integration. Global rather than solely international levels of mismatch can now be determined so that management, having determined its view of interest rates, can establish not only the overall extent of its currency and asset mismatch, but also in which markets it will take these positions.

Despite such progress, however, international bank management continues to face several problems in the management of its overall money dealing functions. In many banks, the management information system is not capable of breaking down the component portions of a deposit and foreign exchange dealing function: the pure matched deposit profit on a back-to-back deposit transaction; the profit derived from a deposit gap or mismatch position; and the pure foreign exchange profit resulting either from favourable movements in spot and forward rates or from a matched transaction. From the standpoint of risk control, many banks still are unable to calculate on a real time basis their global liquidity, interest rate, and foreign exchange exposures. A related concern is the high absolute volume of dealing transactions coupled with the general admission that no control system can totally eliminate the possibility of fraudulent or excessive dealing. While such systems have been imposed over time, one of the continuing risks of the Euro-currency market is the possibility of such dealing losses which occur before management can take appropriate action.

Another problem is that of communication between management and dealers. With the exception of a limited number of individuals who have actually spent several years or more on the trading desk, few international bank managers, from the level of branch manager upward, have a complete understanding of the actual functioning of a dealing room and the nature of the risks and rewards involved in running dealing positions. By the same token, dealers tend to be understandably preoccupied with what is a very high tension, transaction-oriented profession, and often have difficulty in accepting bank policies which may have a negative effect on their own area of operations. In such an environment, there is often a reluctance to be totally open with management if the dealer feels it will impair his ability to perform. Given the vast sums and potential risks involved, improved communications and mutual understanding between the two is of prime importance to senior bank management.

10 Lending Policy: The Management of Risk Assets

The interest differential income and fees from a portfolio of risk assets represent 80 per cent or more of the typical international commercial bank's revenues. From the standpoint of earnings as well as market image, therefore, a bank's lending policy is critical to its global strategy. Efforts to promote non-credit products may enhance a bank's image or relieve some pressure on balance sheet growth, but bank earnings will always correlate highly with the degree of success in improving the risk/reward ratio in lending.

As the typical bank's international portfolio has evolved from virtually riskless short-term loans to medium-term credits involving corporate risks, and eventually to the predominance of long-term loans of a sovereign risk character, there has been a similar evolution of controls over the loan portfolio. One of the principal themes of such controls has been diversification of risk, a traditional banking tenet but one which has special relevance in the international market because of the relative novelty to banks of extensive sovereign risk exposure. The typical international bank will, therefore, have established limits to individual country exposure which will often be broken down further by maturity (short versus medium term), public sector versus private sector, nature of exposure (local currency versus Euro-currency) and so forth. In fixing such limits, banks usually establish some relationship with their own net worth or overall loan portfolio. Similar limits may be applied to specific industries or sectors such as real estate or shipping which carry a perceived level of generic credit risk. Some of the larger and more sophisticated American banks also limit their particular share of bank loans to a given country so as to avoid the vulnerability which might result from being by far the largest lender among overseas banks, should that country have difficulties.

In addition, many banks establish overall loan portfolio guidelines with respect to average loan maturity and the percent of the portfolio which will mature annually so as to ensure a relatively even portfolio run-off. Those banks which engage in fixed rate medium-term lending without the presence of a matching fixed rate deposits generally place overall limits on this form of term mismatch.

The credit decision-making process which has evolved over time reflects the factors of relative bank size and level of international sophistication, the tradition of decision-making within the bank, the personality and influence of key individuals in this process, and past credit experience. One of the distinguishing characteristics of this process is the presence or absence of a credit committee which vets individual exposures prior to approval. The alternative to this collective decision-making process is a delegation of lending authority to individual banking officers in home office and abroad on the basis of their relative position in the organisation and presumed ability to evaluate credits. Most banks provide officers in the field with some delegated lending authority, but in many cases the level of this authority reflects the retail orientation of the bank and is not of an amount – say $1 million or more – sufficient to commit to a typical Euro-currency transaction.

SPECIFIC RESPONSES TO LENDING ISSUES

Of the 38 banks in the 1978 questionnaire sample who expressed a specific view, 25 or roughly two-thirds place primary reliance on a credit committee at either the international or bank-wide level in the organisation, while the remaining third delegate most credit decisions to individuals or use a balanced combination of both. US and Canadian banks tend to rely to a greater extent than others on delegation to individual officers: only 57 per cent of those institutions interviewed used a credit committee extensively, while roughly three-quarters of the non-North American banks did so. Not unexpectedly the institutions which characterised themselves as centralised decision-making structures tended also to rely on credit committees, although in a few instances a centralised bank would rely on individual limits and a decentralised one would use a committee system.

Most banks, in particular the larger ones, tend to have two or more levels of credit decision-making authority whether or not a committee system is utilised. A typical pattern would involve a branch or division manager, the head of international and a bank-wide credit committee each taking the ultimate decision on a credit depending upon its size and nature. The overseas manager might have a $1 million lending limit, and his superior in the international function one of $5 million, above which the credit committee must be consulted. The largest US institutions have generally found it necessary from both the administrative and customer service point of view to delegate significant credit authority to officers abroad. By delegating very substantial lending authority to individuals in direct contact with customers, they hope to minimise the inevitable delays associated with presenting a credit at head office. Non-American banks, however, tend to delegate relatively little authority regardless of their size. Aware of the necessity of providing a quick and constructive response to customers, particularly in a highly competitive market, these banks generally take pride in what they regard as a quick 'turnaround' response to a request for credit. As discussed previously, one-quarter of the banks interviewed cited speed and flexibility of decision-making as the principal element in their business strategy, while the same characteristic was mentioned as one of their three most important strategic elements by a larger number of banks – 28 – than any other priority.

Whether their customers and the banks offering them loan participations would agree that this strategy has been translated into performance, however, is another question. While an international bank – particularly one utilising credit committees – may feel it has provided a timely response, the period before the customer (or agent bank) receives the desired commitment may be delayed considerably because of the need to communicate complete information to the individual in home office who will present the proposal to the committee, requests for clarification or modification from the committee which must be acted upon in the field, delays in bringing the committee together, and similar factors. The initial enthusiasm of the overseas account officer responsible for the proposal may well give the customer or agent bank an unduly positive impression which often disappears when more senior officers have had the opportunity to apply other points of view to the transaction. For traditional relationships and high priority customers, however, even the largest and most centralised institution can probably give a response within a day or so to a fairly straightforward credit request. Should a complex transaction, new country risk, deviation from standard lending policy or similar factor be involved, a substantially longer response time is involved.

The collective credit decision-making process of most continental European and Japanese banks differs significantly from that of the typical North American and British institution. Although some exceptions to this generalisation exist, one can say that the majority of Japanese and European banks utilise part or all of their senior management in the form of a Comité de Direction, Vorstand or similar managing body as a credit committee to make the bulk of their credit decisions. Such a diffuse, collective credit responsibility contrasts sharply with the emphasis on individual credit responsibility characteristic of an American, Canadian or British bank whether or not a credit committee is involved in the final decision.

Informal as well as formal procedures characterise the international credit decision-making process. A German Landesbank, for example, may have an elaborate structure of delegation of authority and required approvals from various bodies through the Board of Directors, but many credit decisions are made informally by a very few individuals who secure retrospective approval from the required bodies as needed. Within a given credit committee or level of individual credit responsibility, the authority of individual officers varies widely. Credit committee meetings may be dominated by a chief executive or a senior bank credit officer, while individual officers, depending on personality, experience and influence within the organisation, may either exceed their nominal authorities without fear of retribution or, on the other hand, consult with superiors on credits well within their authority.

A distinction must also be made between different types of credit. While accustomed to evaluating the creditworthiness of other banks, many institutions with relatively new international functions have had little corporate credit background, with the result that experienced domestic banking officers, either through membership of a bank-wide credit committee or as the final lending authority, become involved when an international corporate credit is presented. In most continental European and Japanese banks which traditionally have had a single (domestic) lending function, this latter continues to make corporate lending decisions even if the customer has been brought in by the international function. Where such lending authority should lie is a subject of some debate among bankers. The larger American banks have built up over time a strong corporate credit capability in their international departments, but smaller institutions in many cases have transferred international corporate lending authority effectively back to domestic officers. Sovereign risk lending is generally the responsibility of international bankers, but in some Japanese, Swiss and other banks this authority resides in a bank-wide lending function. By utilising a bank-wide committee as opposed to one composed of international personnel, management can tailor its approval mechanism to the type of credit involved and the particular strengths and weaknesses of its lending officers.

Another distinction is that of the corporate form of the unit making the credit proposal. Wholly-owned subsidiaries as well as joint ventures and consortium banks tend to receive a greater degree of delegated credit authority than a branch. A number of French, Belgian, American and other banks have utilised wholly-owned subsidiaries rather than branches in overseas markets to perform specific roles, and credit decisions of such institutions may require only a telephoned or telexed approval of a given transaction from home office as opposed to the formal presentation which otherwise might be required.

If a committee system is utilised, it can fulfil a variety of functions in addition to that simply of approving credits. A review committee may evaluate past decisions delegated to individual lending officers on the basis of creditworthiness as well as conformity with bank policy. A credit committee may also set pricing, quality and other lending policies. Finally, it may serve as a vehicle to communicate such policies and to educate officers who are not normally involved in the lending process.

The particular credit decision-making structure chosen by a given bank reflects the latter's overall decision-making approach, which in turn, as previously mentioned, is a function of size and sophistication, the bank's track record, and the personalities and backgrounds of key individuals. A regional bank with a highly domestic-oriented Board of Directors or Chief Executive is quite unlikely to delegate significant credit authority beyond a few trusted individuals, while the same is true of an organisation with a past record of loan losses or other international problems. By the same token, a continental European or Japanese bank with a tradition of collective decision-making in all sectors will probably want to approve most significant credit decisions at the Board of Management level. On the other hand, management with long experience – and frustration – of operating overseas will tend to delegate more to branches and other units.

THE LOSS RECORD IN INTERNATIONAL LENDING

The presumed principal objective of these procedures and guidelines is, of course, the minimisation of international loan losses over the long term. Apart from US banking institutions which are required to disclose detailed information about the loss experience and other features of their international portfolio, few international banks publicly provide such data. Given the relatively limited legal reporting requirements outside the USA and the understandable desire of bankers not to voluntarily advertise past errors, it is unlikely that this situation will change radically in the forseeable future. It is interesting to note, however, that virtually all of the 40 banks interviewed in this questionnaire sample in 1978 reported that their historical international loss experience had been nominal or non-existent and therefore only a fraction of the domestic percentage loss ratio, which tends to confirm the experience of the banks which have actually published their loss performance.

An analysis of the published data on US bank international loan loss experience is, nonetheless, a most useful guide to that of the overall industry. Not only do such banks represent close to one-third of the international lending market, but as the leaders and principal innovators of the Euro-currency sector their portfolios can be expected to be relatively mature and reflect most of the risks currently being assumed by such institutions. Table 10.1 provides a comparison of the 1976–81 international vs. overall loss experience of the major US banks.

In none of the years under review did international loss experience for the ten-bank sample exceed that of the consoli-

TABLE 10.1   International and Consolidated Loan Loss: Experience of Ten Major US Banks in 1976–81

	Net International Loan Losses as % of Foreign Branch Loans	Consolidated Net Losses as % of Total Loans
1976	0.39	0.70
1977	0.32	0.47
1978	0.20	0.32
1979	0.13	0.22
1980	0.11	0.31
1981	0.12	0.25

Note: Arithmetic average of ten largest banks.

Source: Salomon Brothers.

dated average, and during the 1979–81 period international losses on a relative basis represented only one-half or less of the bank-wide percentage.

A more comprehensive analysis of US bank loss experience in 1977 and 1981 is provided in a study by Robert Morris Associates summarised in Table 10.2

While the sample bases differ, the resulting data do confirm

TABLE 10.2   Comparison of Domestic and International Net Loan Charge-offs for US Banks 1977–81

	Net Charge-offs as Percentage of Average Loan Portfolio			
	1977		1981	
	Domestic	International	Domestic	International
1. All reporting banks	0.51	0.18	0.36	0.09
2. Banks with over $5 billion assets	0.58	0.19	0.34	0.09

Note: Banks reporting international losses represent a significantly smaller sample than the domestic category; in 1981, 924 banks reported for the latter vs. 136 for the international category.

Source: Robert Morris Associates.

the relatively good performance of international lending for US institutions. In both 1977 and 1981, international write-offs for the broad-based samples were about one-third to one-quarter of the domestic loss experience. This relatively low level of international losses was confirmed by the non-US banks interviewed, virtually all of whom reported that their historical international losses were not only low in absolute terms but also in comparison with their respective domestic experience.

The limited available data thus suggest that international loss experience through 1981 has been essentially the result of lending to private firms in sectors and countries which have suffered significant structural problems in the mid-1970s and early 1980s: real estate development throughout the world, large crude oil carrier and bulk cargo ships without adequate time charter revenue, and private sector firms whose foreign currency borrowings became significantly more expensive following a major devaluation of the local currency. The Robert Morris survey quoted above also provides a breakdown of the large losses suffered by US banks internationally. Of the total $110 million in 1977, $23 million, or 21 per cent, had been lent to Mexican private sector entities. The next largest loss of $16 million related to UK borrowers, principally real estate developers, while the high ranking of Greece, Panama and Liberia reflects shipping losses.

In 1981 the pattern had changed somewhat. Of the total $316 million in net write-offs, 4 per cent represented loans to government entities as banks wrote off some of their sovereign exposure in Poland, Turkey and Nicaragua. Of the top five countries where losses occurred, two were high inflation economies – Brazil (11 per cent of the total) and Argentina (6 per cent) – whereas the other three were countries where little or no sovereign risk is perceived – the UK (9 per cent), Germany (8 per cent) and Japan (8 per cent).

By the 1980s, one might therefore conclude, US banks were experiencing the negative fall-out of their decision to focus on two categories of private sector overseas borrower: firms in low-risk Western European countries which had sought foreign bank loans to support rapid growth, and companies in high-risk, high-growth Latin American economies which had encountered problems in servicing foreign debt. While such experience does in many respects reflect the peculiar nature of international risk, it can be argued that most of these losses were due to factors which caused similar problems in the respective domestic lending sector – overcapacity, inflation, poor management, depressed prices, and so forth.

OUTLOOK FOR INTERNATIONAL LENDING

It is on the future prospects for loss experience, however, that most international bankers focus their attention. Outside observers have pointed out such obvious potential problems as the extremely heavy relative external debt burdens of many developing countries which are not experienced and tested borrowers, the relative immaturity of many banks' international portfolios where grace periods on principal repayments have often not expired, and the very heavy exposure of the banking community as a whole to adverse developments in a limited number of developing countries.

The 1978 Survey

In this context is is particularly interesting to analyse the responses given in 1978 by the 40-bank sample in connection with the possible extent of future international losses. Of the 31 banks prepared to express a view on the appropriate level of international loan loss reserve for their institution *in the future*, about half considered that a reserve of 0.5 per cent or less of total international loan exposure was appropriate. The remaining half were split roughly between those who considered adequate a reserve of 0.5 – 1.0 per cent and one of 1.0 per cent and above. Non-North American banks tended to be a bit more conservative, with almost three-quarters advocating a reserve of 0.5 per cent or more against only 40 per cent of the North American institutions.

The sovereign risk and/or bank-guaranteed nature of the bulk of their international portfolios was cited almost unanimously as the justification for a relatively low or nominal international reserve. While most international bankers acknowledged that several smaller sovereign borrowers may go into open default and possibly bring about losses of interest or even principal to the lenders, the point was made that private sector borrowers, both domestic and international, have historically represented far greater risks of actual loss. Many of those interviewed were thus prepared for an increase in the international loss ratio, although only a few felt it would approach domestic levels.

An outside evaluation of the overall international position of a bank's balance sheet is also hindered by the relative lack of publicly-available data. Only US and Canadian institutions among the major countries provide a breakdown of international assets and liabilities as well as earnings contribution and relative margins. In appraising such vital factors as level of leverage or gearing, liquidity and the ratio of loans to deposits, however, it can be argued that it is irrelevant and artificial to break out the international component of a balance sheet in what is essentially an integrated international institution.

What is of relevance to the management of such institutions, however, is the relative importance of the international component of a bank's earnings and assets. The growth of such aggregates in percentage terms has been impressive enough; but in addition slow growth or stagnation in domestic earnings plus severe domestic setbacks in individual cases have caused the international contribution of earnings to rise in many cases to 50 per cent or more of the bank's total. Of the 34 banks in the 1978 questionnaire sample who calculate the overall profit contribution of the international function (six do not or do not feel it is relevant), about one-third show an international contribution ranging from 10–20 per cent of the total, with another fifth in the 30–40 per cent category. Four, or roughly 12 per cent, had an international contribution exceeding 50 per cent of the total. The higher levels have been achieved by the larger US banks which have suffered from flat domestic earnings for many years as well as other banks with major domestic earnings problems.

Of the 37 institutions prepared in 1978 to hazard an opinion, roughly two-thirds anticipated an increase in their percentage of international earnings over the medium term. About half of the North American banks polled forecast such an increase, while only two of the other seventeen institutions foresaw a decrease in the percentage. There was no particular correlation between the existing level of international contribution and the forecast. Those predicting further relative growth usually foresaw fairly unattractive domestic expansion prospects, while many of those predicting a decline had in mind a recovery or continuation of domestic loan demand. American banks were not optimistic about future international growth because of the relatively unattractive risk/reward ratio prevalent in mid-1978 in the Euro-currency market and the corresponding relative attractiveness of domestic lending. On the other hand, the more optimistic bankers in many cases reflected the amortisation of heavy past expenses of building up their international function which should produce, in the future, more attractive profits.

A very interesting issue is that of whether a limit should be placed on the earnings or asset contribution of the international function to the global bank. Of 34 banks which responded to this query, somewhat less than half saw no need for such a policy determination; they essentially believed that a pragmatic approach should be taken with regard to the relative risk and reward of international business. On the other hand, a small majority felt that considerations of external perception (the stock market, customers, regulatory authorities, etc.) required that the international contribution be limited to a certain percentage of the total. For many European banks, such a constraint stemmed from a desire to be seen to retain a national character or a given domestic market share, while many US institutions are concerned about their image with investors and customers. A frequent maximum contribution cited by many American regional banks is that of one-third of total profits and assets. Many European bankers interviewed criticised US institutions for reaching a level of international earnings which could result in a possible loss of identity, while others have in mind the more material concern of diversification of assets and earnings.

The Group of Thirty 1981 survey

The more extensive survey of lending policy carried out in 1981 by the Group of Thirty reflects a significant change in risk perception.[1]

Noting that foreign assets as a percentage of the total had risen from 12 per cent to 22 per cent during the decade of the 1970s, the study concluded that concern over country risk had increased and that there was more scepticism over banks' ability to evaluate country risk. Forty per cent of the banks interviewed anticipated a substantial increase in the riskiness of international lending during the next five years. Indicative of the banks' difficulty in evaluating such risk was the continued primary reliance on diversification of risk as the principal risk control technique. The study also pointed up the relative absence of factual information on debt service and the fact that

> competition for business ... has sometimes resulted in excessive debt accumulation by borrowers, leading subsequently to debt servicing problems.[2]

The report concludes that 'rescheduling will be a recurrent feature of the international financial system of the 1980s'.[3]

When the study was written, 11 country reschedulings had taken place or were in process; these have since been joined by Mexico, Ecuador, Argentina and others.

Other Issues

One lending policy issue of increasing relevance is the trade-off between specialisation and diversification. As banks move towards specialist lending products in their efforts to add value and increase the reward from lending, there is often a corresponding or greater reliance on a geographic or functional sector whose problems can have a disproportionate impact on the bank's earning power.

In terms of functional specialisation, in virtually all of the sectors which have attracted international bank interest in the late 1970s and early 1980s, problems peculiar to those sectors have resulted in a sharp increase in non-performing loans. Shipping, aerospace, real estate and energy over this period are sectors in which banks have invested considerable human and financial resources; each in turn has been afflicted with problems. Individual banks specialising in these sectors have certainly emerged successfully from these cyclical downturns, but in other cases disproportionate losses have been suffered both by newcomers and well-established lenders to these markets. In terms of geographic specialisation, Poland's problems have been a particular burden to Austrian and German banks who found Eastern European lending a natural focus, while some American and other banks are heavily reliant on certain Latin American countries such as Argentina and Mexico in which they have had a long and hitherto profitable local and foreign currency lending activity.

Finally there are also severe limitations to the use of expertise to add value to credit as well as non-credit products. Project financing, in the sense of assuming a non-recourse project risk in exchange for a higher reward to the lender, offers interesting profit opportunities for a bank prepared to assume these risks. On the other hand, there is only a finite number of bankable projects, which will not necessarily increase with the number of banks theoretically interested in financing them. Moreover, the incremental fees and loan spreads obtained may pale in the face of the losses suffered from a drastic commodity price decrease or other unforeseen event. Whether the bank acts as an advisor or lender to such a project, it is difficult to avoid the conclusion that only a limited number of international banks will have the expertise and opportunity to benefit from the number of available opportunities.

11 Organisational Structure

Having selected the appropriate mix of clients, markets and products as well as overseas network, the international bank must then select an organisational and decision-making structure which is most appropriate for the chosen strategy. This chapter will describe the organisational alternatives available, the considerations which lie behind the selection of a particular structure, and how the organisation actually functions in terms of the decision-making process.

THE THREE ORGANISATIONAL DIMENSIONS

As already discussed, the three critical dimensions of product, client and market are inevitably reflected in a bank's organisational structure. The critical difference is the relative importance assigned to each of the three dimensions.

A product orientation relates to specific products or groups of products provided to clients. Typical product groups around which an organisation can be structured are treasury, capital market/merchant banking, correspondent banking/institutional services, export/trade finance and financial advisory. Specific internally oriented services such as planning, data processing and marketing are also essentially organised on a product basis. Such a service-oriented structure facilitates individual and profit accountability and inevitably represents a significant portion of most banks' international organisational structure because of the indivisibility of the functions involved.

A geographic structure, on the other hand, focuses on a specific regional orientation, such as the Far East, Americas, Europe, and so forth. By organising part or all of its international function along geographic lines, a bank assumes that the commonality of business conditions in a given region and its own expertise in these areas is of more organisational relevance than the products offered or customer requirements in the particular geographic region. This territorial orientation is perhaps the

126

most traditional form of organisation among international banks in that it reflects the prototype international function which was built around foreign correspondent bank relationships and the financing of short-term trade flows. At a minimum, all banks offer at least a portion of their international services under a geographic designation.

Finally the third dimension is based on the category of customer or client relationship. This can be of the generic variety – say, corporate, bank or retail – or related to specific industry or sectoral groupings which have perceived common requirements and characteristics. As international banks have come to grips with the greater sophistication of non-bank customers and their requirements, an increasing number have begun to orient their structure towards servicing such particular needs. What began, for example, as a specialist staff function providing technical services for lending officers working with the oil or shipping industries, became a line function with responsibility for the energy or transportation sectors. A logical next step was to create similar line responsibility for other customer groups – governmental, chemicals, forest products, and so on – on a sectoral basis. With such a client focus, the international function in many respects becomes a support activity. For banks which found such a detailed segmentation too inflexible or unnecessary, broader categories such as multinational, consumer and national may be more relevant. In practice, this customer orientation is effectively a combination of the product/functional and territorial form of organisation using the customer as the focal point. It can also be argued that this third format is nothing more than a particular combination of the original two in that there is a unique balance between territorial and product considerations with the customer representing the focal point of that balance. Consequently, this can be regarded as a swing towards functionalism, in that geographic expertise in the form of the international department simply becomes another function along with, say, investment banking activities, rather than a self-standing bank within a bank.

TYPICAL ORGANISATIONAL STRUCTURES

In practice, every international function is organised with varying elements of several of these three structures. What differs is the relative degree of emphasis on each in the organisational chart as well as such factors as the influence of particular individuals in the organisation, the physical size of the bank, the traditional characteristics of a given bank's business and the willingness to make major organisational changes to maximise profits or provide better customer services. The most prevalent and traditional structure is one based on territorial or geographic lines with certain separate functional groups reporting to the same senior officer. Thus most of the bank's customer-oriented lending and service activities would be grouped as in Figure 11.1 on a regional basis, with internally-oriented functions such as money dealing and staff services organised functionally. There is, therefore, a clear differentiation between the domestic and international functions of the bank at the operating and customer level, while within the international function individual territories would exist relatively independently of each other. The structure shown in Figure 11.1 is typical of most American banks. Obviously the larger institutions have a greater degree of complexity and number of functions, but the essential components are generally common to most US banks.

This type of structure, in which the international function not only funds part or all of its requirements, but also makes its own credit decisions, clearly creates a 'bank within a bank' orientation and mentality. American and other institutions which are organised along these lines believe that the nature of international business is so distinct from that carried on domestically that the risks of separate development and poor communications are relatively unimportant.

The other traditional structural form is that utilised primarily by Japanese and continental European banks which have an international department organised along territorial lines but without the extent of functional responsibility prevalent in US institutions. In many respects, such a global organisational form is essentially functional with the international department charged primarily with the function of dealing with overseas banks and financing international trade. Unlike the structures described in Figure 11.1, such key functions as customer lending and treasury/money dealing are centralised on a bank-wide basis outside the international function. Such a relatively functional and centralised organisation is described in Figure 11.2.

The Japanese, European and other banks which utilise this

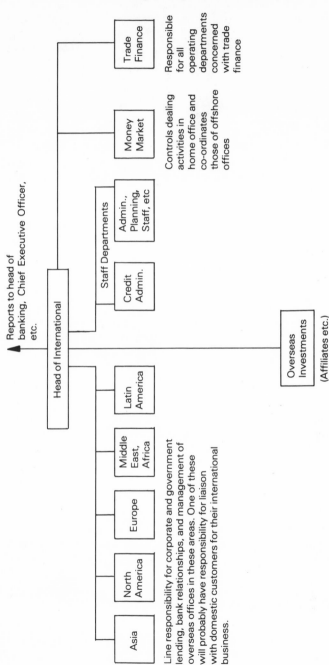

FIGURE 11.1   Typical Territorial/Regional Organisation Chart for International Banks

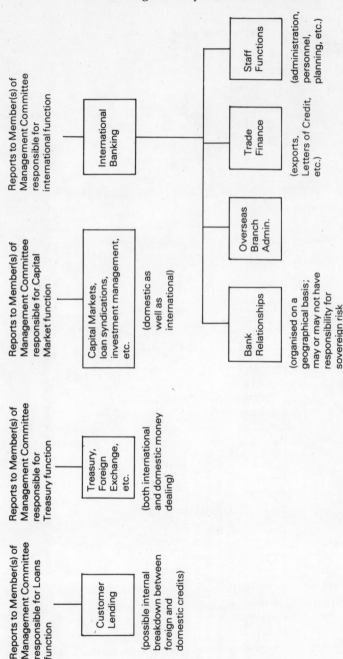

FIGURE 11.2   Typical Functional/Centralised Organisation Chart for International Banks

type of organisational format thus require a considerable extent of functional interaction when dealing with an international corporate customer's loan request, an overseas branch money market problem, a participation in a syndicated credit or similar transaction. Most of the bank's sophisticated credit skills tend to be centralised in the customer lending function which may or may not also have responsibility for vetting sovereign risk exposure, so that its views on a lending transaction involving an international department customer must be solicited. The same type of dotted line or functional relationship may be involved when an overseas branch responsible to the international banking function takes a mismatch or foreign exchange position, or when a branch manager is offered a participation in a syndicated loan to a customer in his own market area.

Efforts to create an optimum balance between a functional/product and geographic orientation have led to what is known as the matrix organisation, developed by several leading American institutions, whereby functional and geographic specialisation are each given deliberate emphasis on a bank-wide basis, to ensure appropriate communications within the bank and to improve customer service by bringing to bear a totality of different specialist functions. Under such a scheme as carried to its logical extreme, for example, every customer of the bank falls into a certain industry or sectoral category and is serviced on a line basis by a specialist in that category. At the same time, a geographic and/or product-oriented group of specialists interacts with the customer specialists to provide staff support. By assigning primary customer responsibility to an industry specialist, such banks tend to break down or even eliminate the historic distinction between domestic and international in their efforts to adapt to the perceived requirements of the multinational corporations. Primary customer responsibility can also be given to a geographic specialist with a knowledge of that customer's base of operations; in turn, he is able to call on a wide range of specialist knowledge throughout the bank to service his customers' needs. In its ideal form, a customer would have at his service perhaps three types of specialist bankers – one who was intimately familiar with his sector and had overall responsibility, another who offered individual products such as money management services, and a third who had a detailed knowledge of the geographic areas of interest to the client.

Figure 11.3 describes a typical matrix organisational structure.

More typically, individual bank organisations in practice tend to fall between the simplified, archetypal organisational forms described above. Rather than adopt a pure matrix or functional approach, many banks utilise a variant by which certain customers or types of customers are serviced by line officers outside the traditional domestic–international organisational structure without actually eliminating that particular distinction. A specific customer group – say energy-related customers or large multinational firms – would be split out from the straightforward domestic–international organisation and covered on a line or staff basis by specialists in that group. Quite often such a compromise variant represents a transition towards the full matrix structure from the traditional geographic orientation.

The comprehensive international functions of US and UK banks which group all possible internationally oriented activities are, in effect, the ultimate territorial organisation. On the other hand, the continental European or Japanese structure is strongly product-oriented in the sense that international is viewed as a specific product or function along with corporate lending, capital markets and money market activities which are carried on with little territorial distinction.

FACTORS INFLUENCING ORGANISATIONAL STRUCTURE

Whether recognised explicitly or implicitly, a bank's strategy determines its organisational structure. One dimension of this relationship is the bank's position on the international life cycle. In phase 1, a limited number of international products are made available in a geographic framework based on correspondent relationships. Treasury and credit products may be the province of a domestic function. A trend towards the product and client dimensions occurs in phases 2 and 3 as the bank offers a larger and more sophisticated range of products, builds an international treasury capability and widens its target client range. The traditional domestic/international geographic organisational split becomes blurred as functional groups based on product or client categories are established: merchant banking functions which handle loan syndication and advisory products; multina-

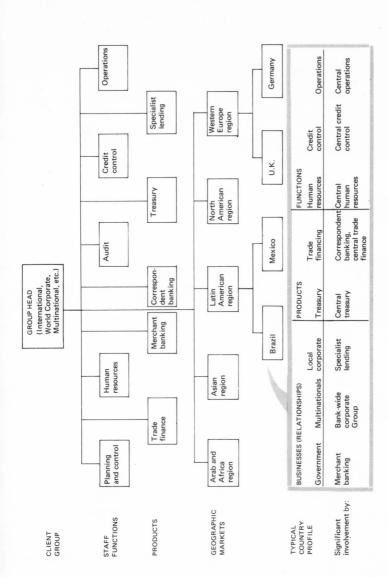

FIGURE 11.3 Sample Matrix Organisational Structure

tional banking groups; specialist lending functions and the like. Phase 4 represents the sharpest delineation of all three dimensions. The extreme is a formal three-dimensional matrix organisation, while at a minimum each dimension will be acknowledged by the fixing of product, market and client responsibilities with a specific bias towards one or more of these dimensions.

Within this framework, the choice of a strategic direction should have a decisive impact on the organisational structure selected. A bank focusing on delivering high valued-added, specialist products should give organisational prominence to the highly skilled professionals capable of providing these services. A decentralised structure is most appropriate for such a strategy. One with traditional strength in specific geographic regions through an extensive branch network will understandably give preference to the geographic dimension, while a conservative bank defending market share is more likely to adopt a highly centralised structure.

In practice, the actual choice of organisational structure reflects a variety of factors which may or may not form part of a conscious, deliberate strategy. While an ideal structure derived from a strategic plan may be put on paper, in the real world a critical role is played by the physical size of the bank, the influence and background of key individuals in senior management, the bank's historical development in the international market, and the nature of its existing domestic and international business.

Size is a key determinant of organisation, not only because of the physical resources which a larger bank can bring to bear, but also because of the problems of such an organisation in responding efficiently and effectively to the needs of customers as well as staff. For a far-flung, world-wide organisation offering hundreds of services to thousands of customers from dozens of branches and offices throughout the world, movement towards a matrix-type organisation may be a necessary step to avoid either administrative chaos or the inability to bring to bear the specific expertise needed by a particular customer. By the same token, only the larger organisations can afford the expense of highly paid staffs of customer, product and geographic specialists.

The human factor is also an essential determinant of organisational structure. An individual or individuals who have built a large and profitable international function over a period of decades are unlikely, in the absence of significant outside pressures, to completely remodel the structure which they fashioned and which has become the basis of their influence in the bank.

On the other hand, the arrival of a new chief executive or head of international – particularly one from outside the organisation – or a reorganisation within the international function, may well offer the opportunity to change a structure to meet the requirements of the new management and/or the needs of the marketplace. The background of the leadership of an international function is also important. A traditional international banker oriented towards relationships with other bankers is naturally inclined towards a structure with a primarily geographic basis, while a newcomer with experience outside the banking industry may be more prone to orient international functions along customer or product lines.

Finally the nature and historic evolution of a bank's traditional business is also a major determinant of a particular organisational structure. A bank with historical ties to, or a major branch network in a given region is unlikely to give up entirely its geographic orientation, while a relative newcomer to the international scene may be more inclined to specialise in particular customer groups or services which are seen to be attractive at the present time. Such a newcomer might even wish to dispense with the traditional global orientation, which subsumes activity throughout the world and the necessity of a desk officer for each country in the world, in favour of a more pragmatic, targeted approach oriented towards high potential areas and functions. By the same token, a bank with its domestic origins in a particular speciality – say a US regional bank with a petroleum industry orientation or a Swiss bank with an investment management tradition – will probably choose an international structure which reflects this dominant domestic emphasis. Such a traditional functional commitment often requires a global management orientation as opposed to what can be regarded as an artificial distinction between domestic and international operations.

Given the evolution of external forces and the response to them of individual banks, it is hardly surprising that many organisational structures are in a period of flux or transition and that banks' senior managements are often dissatisfied with the performance of current structures. In the first place, particularly among larger banks, there are serious problems of reconciling, on the one hand, size and complexity of structure with, on the other hand, flexibility and responsiveness to needs of staff and customers. While a matrix-type organisation for a large bank can be intellectually satisfying on paper, in practice the necessary interaction and communication among a number of individuals from different parts of the organisation, each of which has some kind of responsibility for the relationship, can lead to significant delays in the decision-making process, frustration on the part of bank officers who feel they spend more time relating to other officers in the bank than in actually doing the business which interests them, and in the end the lack of responsive and constructive customer services for which the organisation was designed. On the other hand, smaller banks, or those without the array of specialist talents and products, find it increasingly difficult to compete for the business of customers who have substantial and sophisticated requirements with a global orientation.

Major American banks have been prominent in the search for an organisational structure which best fits the constraints imposed by large size, the need to motivate and mobilise efficiently highly skilled specialists, and the global requirements of corporate customers. Such banks have moved, for example, from a domestic/international split to a world corporate/domestic distinction to a corporate/retail structure in an effort to find the right balance. Whatever distinction is made in terms of client breakdown, however, there remains the problem of effectively mobilising and motivating product and transaction-oriented specialists who are frustrated by the constraints in a multi-dimensional structure of co-ordinating with a variety of other areas of the bank. An example of the effort devoted to resolve internal stresses at the possible expense of generating revenues is shown by the senior Citibank merchant banker whose 'Number one job is to make sure we work with the [Citibank] institution rather than to find clients.'[1]

Secondly, organisational structures are invariably hampered by a shortage of key personnel who possess the appropriate ingredients of management skills, credit judgement, business development talent and specialist expertise. Such an increasing gap between supply and demand for human resources is understandable in an industry which has grown enormously in physical size as well as number of participants. The opening up of a new offshore financial centre, for example, not only increases demand for more branch managers, more staff support in home office and more systems to handle the increased volume of business, but also brings to the scene entirely new institutions formed to exploit that particular market. Placing the title of branch manager or private placement specialist after the name of an individual does not necessarily endow him with the requisite talents, and organisational structures must often be modified to reflect such weaknesses.

In the early 1980s the larger and more sophisticated banks face two critical organisational issues. The first is the conflict between the need to market high value, transaction-based products and the organisational constraints imposed by the vertical and complex structure of the typical international commercial bank. Their competitors in such product areas are horizontally structured, flexible institutions such as the British merchant banks and US investment banks which are not burdened by matrix-type reporting requirements, account officer responsibilities and relatively structured compensation arrangements. The record of US and other commercial banks in attracting and retaining such high performance individuals is not good.

The second issue is a growing dissatisfaction with the complex matrix organisation which tends to contribute to the problem discussed above as well as restrain individual initiative, lengthen response time and make it more difficult to identify responsibility. The growing use of account officers, who have overall responsibility for particular client relationships, represents an effort to resolve this problem of complexity, but the responses to the surveys described in Chapter 7 highlight the difficulties banks have in putting in place an adequate group of relationship officers with sufficient experience, continuity and relevant skills. As banks move away from a balanced matrix with two or three dimensions which are relatively equal in importance, there has been a trend toward focus on a single dimension – usually geographic – which dominates the decision-making structure. In many cases, this amounts to a return to the 'Fiefdoms' or 'baronies' of an earlier structure where the country or regional head dominated all aspects of the bank's business in that particular market.

SPECIFIC ORGANISATIONAL RESPONSES

When asked to characterise their existing organisational structure in these terms, 31, or over 80 per cent of the 37 banks responding in 1978 considered their structures to be primarily geographic in orientation. The remaining one-sixth of the total, which includes primarily larger US banks, regarded their approach as more functionally or matrix-oriented with a balance between geographical and functional specialisation. Another one-sixth of the total, which presently considers itself primarily geographic in focus, is moving towards a more functional orientation.

The matrix or balanced functional/geographic orientation is principally an American phenomenon, but several of the non-American banks are moving in this direction. Those banks which are most enthusiastic about matrix management tend to be the largest institutions which have a real problem in what one banker called 'the management of size'. With a matrix structure, primary customer responsibility can be given either to a product specialist – say the bank's chemicals expert for a foreign chemical company – or the geographic specialist – say the branch manager in the country in which that particular chemical company is located. Thus in any given matrix organisation one orientation – geographic, functional or customer – must dominate to a certain extent to produce effective results.

Most banks, however, consider that such a matrix system is too complex, disruptive for customer relationships and expensive for their particular organisation to implement. To achieve the desired result of improved internal co-ordination and customer service, other approaches are preferred. One is to select a specific group of customers whose business will be handled outside the traditional territorial organisation; another is to have both the international and domestic departments report to the same senior officer who can, therefore, ensure that appropriate co-ordination takes place. A final approach is to designate an individual or group within the domestic or international function which has co-ordinating responsibility for assisting an account officer in another function.

In addition to improving co-ordination and maximising the level and breadth of expertise applied to a customer's problems, movement towards a functional orientation is justified by many bankers because it enables them to develop and market new and existing products and services, which might not otherwise be the case in a purely geographical structure. As such areas of specialist expertise are developed in the bank's effort to differentiate its product line, they are established as functional units with specific profit responsibility reporting to a senior international officer. For the same reasons, existing specialist services may be taken out of a territorial organisation and given separate reporting channels to the head of international.

In terms of relationship with the domestic functions of their bank, roughly one-quarter of the 40 institutions interviewed have some form of customer line responsibility which cuts across the domestic–international distinction. Of the nine banks which have such a structure, six are North American. Most banks confirmed that the decision to modify their traditional structure was a highly political one, involving the areas of responsibility of key management officers, and that the question of appropriate structures was reviewed frequently. It is interesting to note that the presence of a matrix organisation does not necessarily imply the existence of a multinational or other group which cuts across traditional geographic lines; several banks have established bank-wide functional responsibilities without modifying the basic geographic breakdown between domestic and international customers. Banks which are relatively new to corporate lending both domestically and internationally find co-ordination problems relatively simple to resolve, while those which have substantial and long standing corporate lending business tend to be reluctant to reshuffle customer account responsibilities.

One of the dominant impressions gained from conversations with senior bankers is the absence of total satisfaction with any given organisational structure and the constant search for an appropriate blend of geographic, functional and customer orientation. The problem of reconciling a large and complex organisation with such factors as customer objectives, profit accountability and staff job satisfaction is a considerable one, which is complicated by considerations of personalities and the entrenched positions of key individuals in a given organisation.

FUNCTIONING OF THE ORGANISATION

The actual functioning of a given organisation in terms of decision-making structure is the second focus of this chapter. The vital decisions in international banking relate to credit, staffing, pricing, product, marketing, network, asset and liability structure and other factors, but given the nature and tradition of banking the credit decision-making process tends to assume a position of prominence. Quite apart from the obvious importance of credit quality to a bank's performance, most banks are managed by professional bankers who have risen in the organisation through an extended period of exposure to the lending process, and may be unlikely to voluntarily disassociate themselves from the process, whatever their level of responsibility.

In differentiating the various approaches to decision-making in international banks, two distinctions can be made. Firstly, banks differ in the extent of centralisation of decision-making with particular reference to the credit process. Secondly, they can also be characterised by the degree of diffusion of the decision-making process among individuals at various levels of the organisation.

THE ISSUE OF CENTRALISATION

The extent of centralisation of the process is reflected in both formal and informal organisational charts. At one extreme is the highly centralised organisation where most credit and other decisions are made by one or more individuals in home office with officers in the field used primarily to develop proposals and implement home office decisions. At the other extreme is a decentralised organisation where most business decisions are delegated to officers in the field with direct customer and market contact while home office functions primarily to determine strategy and policy, provide staff services and operating guidelines to regional or local operations and solve problems as they arise.

The choice of degree of centralisation is usually determined by the factors of size and complexity of structure, the background and orientation of senior bank and international management, the nature of the bank's business and the availability of qualified and trusted personnel. A very large bank with a highly complex organisational structure may find it virtually impossible to function competitively without delegating most credit and other decisions to individuals or committees who can provide a timely and constructive response to a customer. On the other hand, equally large banks with more traditional and simplified forms of territorial or product structure can funnel virtually all significant business decisions to a core of senior headquarters personnel which provides a more or less efficient response to officers in the field. In the former category are principally the larger US banks with a complex, matrix-type organisational structure, while in the more centralised category are the great majority of European, Canadian and Japanese banks which traditionally have made credit and other decisions centrally. While size thus does not necessarily determine degree of centralisation, complexity of structure does play a significant role.

The background and orientation of senior management is also important in that a tradition of decades of centralised decision-making in a given institution is extremely difficult to modify. Such a tradition may reflect the lack of familiarity or 'comfort' of senior management with international business, past problems which have placed an indelible imprint on organisational behaviour, or simply the combination of habit and self-interest which perpetuates management practices over an extended period of time. Once again, a radical change in management personalities or outside circumstances may force an equivalent modification of the degree of centralisation.

The nature of a bank's business influences centralisation in several ways. A bank with a large amount of retail or locally-oriented business in foreign countries is likely to have a significant degree of decentralised decision-making, while one with a limited number of large, wholesale loan decisions or with a central core of specialist knowledge in, say, the energy sector is more likely to bring decisions back to home office. The availability and personal objectives of qualified staff are also vital considerations. The traditional justification for centralisation of decision-making is the relative absence of such human skills and the consequent need to concentrate credit and other decisions in home office where the experienced individuals are likely to be located. On the other hand, several American banks have made the opposite argument in recent years by placing their limited supply of experienced staff in the field, in regional headquarters, where they can make more responsive, market-related judgements. Of growing force in recent years has been the frustration of overseas or market-oriented officers in centralised organisations where the individual acquires management or customer-related skills in a foreign environment but is not permitted, in his view, sufficient decision-making authority to match these skills. This problem is compounded by the physical difficulty of communicating to the decision-makers in a far-off home or regional office the background to, and reasons for, a particular credit or other decision which he is proposing.

Such a possible conflict between the field and home office is inevitable in any international organisation, but the problem is particularly acute in international banking because of the importance of the credit decision-making process and the relative lack of experience of so many international bankers in this rapidly developing market. A particular characteristic of recent years among some US banks, therefore, has been the increasing degree of decentralisation as the banks mature internationally and overseas-based staff return to more senior management positions in home office, where they are in a position to correct what they regarded as an overcentralised structure when overseas.

It is interesting to note that length and extent of experience internationally is not a major factor in determining the extent of centralisation. Some of the most experienced international institutions are the most centralised, while some relative newcomers have made the boldest decentralisation moves.

Management Responses to Centralisation

Of the 40 banks interviewed in the 1978 sample, only 13, or one-third, regarded their decision-making process as essentially decentralised, with the balance basically centralised in nature. Roughly the same ratio of centralised versus decentralised structures were shown by the North American sub-sample and the other institutions. A number of relatively centralised banks expressed the desire to delegate more authority but have been restrained by factors such as the traditional decision-making process within the bank, a perceived shortage of experienced bankers in the field, and the record of past mistakes stemming from delegation of authority. The relative predominance of centralised decision-making indicated by the above sample may actually be understated in the sense that several bankers described themselves as decentralised by virtue of the existence of relatively low credit authorities of, say, $500,000 delegated to the field but admitted that most credit and other decisions were made at home office.

Some of the large American banks take pride in the ability of key officers overseas to make substantial commitments, often up to the bank's legal lending limit, without reference to home office. Other large banks which make such decisions centrally pointed out that their 'turnaround time', or response time, for a credit proposal was rapid enough to offset this apparent disadvantage. Among the smaller banks and those with little international experience, it is accepted that a limited number of very senior officers in home office, often including the bank's chief executive officer, will make all substantive credit, personnel, lending policy and other decisions.

The presence or absence of an overseas regional headquarters does not necessarily imply a corresponding delegation of authority except in purely administrative or staff functions. Many European and Japanese banks which have a domestic retail banking tradition and a collegiate form of management decision-making are quite reluctant to delegate authority, even within home office for wholesale lending decisions, which represent for them not only a considerable commitment, but also a radical change in their collective decision-making process.

Whatever the degree of centralisation, the decision-making process usually involves several levels of management. The typical procedure is to delegate at least a minimum of credit and non-credit authority to branch managers or other senior overseas officers – perhaps authority to commit from $500,000 to $5 million equivalent to a given customer depending on the size of the bank and its degree of centralisation. Commitments above this amount would go to a higher authority in the international function in a regional headquarters or in home office, while in many cases a third tier of authority outside the international function – perhaps including the chief executive or chief credit officer – might be required. Outside the realm of credit, decision-making tends to be even more centralised as decisions involving personnel, compensation, lending policy, asset and liability management and other issues tend to involve enough elements in the organisation, or represent a sufficiently important policy decision, to require some form of central approval.

In all this procedure, informal processes are as important as those laid out in the organisational chart. For example, an officer overseas may have a formal delegation to commit to a particular decision, but if he senses that such a decision might not be well received by a higher authority he may not make it without some informal checkings within the organisation. On the other hand, without a formal delegation, individual officers in market-related positions often make what are in effect commitments to customers and others and are able, by virtue of their personality, track record or personal influence with senior management, to implement those commitments. The presence of a formal decision-making process thus may or may not involve a significant review of the particular decision in view of the importance of the confidence factor; proposals of a trusted subordinate may be waved through while those of a less experienced individual or one who does not have his superior's total confidence will be critically reviewed.

The importance of the informal management processes is brought out by a question in the 40-bank survey which asked whether a written organisation chart existed for the international function. While it is dangerous to read too much into the specific responses, it is interesting that over one-third of the total sample did not have available such a chart. Perhaps more remarkable is the fact that almost one-half of the US and Canadian banks, which are known for their focus on individual responsibility and authority, fell into this category. Reasons given for the lack of a readily available organisation chart included the fact that it was in the process of being revised and that it did not reflect the true allocation of responsibilities. At a minimum, these responses confirm the importance of informal relationships in the typical bank decision-making structure.

THE ISSUE OF DIFFUSION OF AUTHORITY AND RESPONSIBILITY

The other distinguishing feature of a decision-making process is the diffusion of authority and responsibility among individuals in the organisational structure. Such diffusion may be measured by the number of individuals involved in a given decision and is characterised by the distinction between individual and group, or committee, responsibility. At one extreme is the typical American bank structure where one senior individual has responsibility for the entire international function and reports to a single member of the senior management of the bank. The head of international in turn delegates specific responsibility for individual products and territories to individuals who each have a clearly defined profit responsibility together with individual decision-making authority. Such a function is relatively formal, structured and compartmentalised, with emphasis on definition of individual responsibility and authority.

At the other extreme is the highly diffuse continental European or Japanese approach where several senior individuals, usually members of a senior management committee which effectively manages the bank, have responsibility for individual aspects of the bank's international business. While an international department exists, this usually encompasses primarily the traditional bank-to-bank and trade-financing business on a territorial basis. Other key functions such as corporate lending, capital market activities and money dealing are the ultimate responsibility of one or more members of the senior management committee, who ordinarily cover both the domestic and international aspects of that particular function. Such a senior management group meets frequently to make most significant – and sometimes minor – credit and other decisions. While a junior credit committee of international personnel may also exist, it is this senior management committee sitting in effect as a credit committee which ultimately makes most credit decisions. Japanese and continental European banks thus tend to have a collective, flexible and interactive management approach without the emphasis on individual responsibility and authority prevalent among US institutions. In some cases, one notes a trend away from shared responsibility in the former type of organisation towards increasing specialisation; the international function, for one, may be assigned to one or more members of the senior management committee as it becomes a larger and more complex aspect of the business.

Diffusion of specific responsibility for credit decisions can exist in any structure through the use of a credit committee, which represents the standard process for most international banks. Those with single international heads as well as senior committee management usually make use of a group decision-making process at various levels for credit approvals. The size, composition and influence of such a committee depends upon the influence of individual personalities as well as the objectives of the committee. One or more individuals such as the chief executive, the head of the credit function or a senior international officer may dominate the committee and its proceedings. In addition to actually making credit decisions, the committee may serve also as an educational and communications forum for individuals not directly involved in the credit process. A variety of titles – Credit Allocation, Loan/Credit Policy, Asset/Liability Management, etc. – is used for what can range from simply rubber stamping a past credit approval to making broad policy decisions covering pricing, lending policy, personal, network management and other factors.

The use of a relatively diffuse process reflects a variety of factors, including a perceived lack of qualifications of individual banking officers, historical decision-making tradition on a group basis, and a natural tendency among bankers to become and remain part of the essential credit decision-making process. In countries such as Japan where business decisions are traditionally made from the bottom up on a collective basis, such a process is quite natural. In continental European banks which have always been run by a mangement committee on a collegiate basis and where senior management may not yet be comfortable with international exposure, the same is true. On the other hand, in American institutions where individual effort and accountability are features of business life, diffusion of the decision-making process is more limited and takes the form primarily of a credit review committee, which often only ratifies decisions already taken in practice, or exists primarily for communication or educational purposes.

A relatively diffuse decision-making structure has the obvious advantage of bringing to bear the combined wisdom of a large number of interested and experienced individuals, as well as communicating policy and practice to a wide range of officers. On the other hand, by its nature it may significantly hamper individual initiative and accountability, in particular as the natural tendency of any group decision is to impose terms and conditions important to individuals in the group but possibly of little value in the real competitive world. The committee process is particularly difficult in international banking where not only may several committee members have little international experience, but also where propositions must often be supported by an individual who has ultimate responsibility but who cannot be physically present to defend his proposal.

In countries such as the USA and UK with a single tier Board of Directors, such a body is rarely involved in day-to-day lending or other decisions, but rather functions in a review or audit capacity and in the approval of strategic decisions such as acquisitions or major expansion moves. The same is generally true of the top Board (Aufsichtsrat, Conseil d'Administration, etc.) of continental European and Japanese banks which also have a second or operating Board (Vorstand, Direction Générale, Board of General Managers, Board of Managing Directors, etc.). It is the latter, however, which plays the dominant role in the more diffuse and flexible decision-making structure in such countries. The role of the chief executive officer in the day-to-day decision-making process varies considerably throughout the world, with little correlation as to country. Some chief executives continue to involve themselves in day-to-day customer-related and other decisions, while others have restricted themselves to a policy-making role.

An effort was made to quantify the extent to which banks in the questionnaire sample had a single head of international with responsibility for all international business including credit decision-making authority and Euro-currency money market operations. Of the 40 banks, 29 or roughly three-quarters described their structure in such terms, while in the remaining quarter several different members of senior management were responsible for various aspects of overseas business. In reality, however, the latter number is probably understated as many banks with supposedly one head of international have centralised either corporate credit authority or the global treasury function outside the area of responsibility of this individual. With very few exceptions, however, the 21 US and Canadian banks interviewed did centralise all these aspects of their international activities under one individual. Of the non-North American banks, therefore, somewhat over one-half claimed to have a single head of all international operations.

In the instances where a true single head of the international function exists, he tends to report to a single member of senior management who is either the head of banking (or corporate banking), the chief executive of the bank, or another member of top management. Of the 29 instances in the sample of a single international head, in ten cases he reported directly to the chief executive officer of the bank, in eight instances to the head of banking or corporate banking, and in three cases to an executive management committee.

12 Implementing The Strategy: Systems and Human Resource Issues

Having established its business strategy along with the appropriate network and organisational structure, international bank management must deal with a variety of issues in actually implementing the chosen strategy. In large part, such issues revolve around two types of resource: systems and people. The bank's operating systems produce relevant data for planning and management information as well as the means by which banking transactions are processed and accounting information developed. Its human resources must be recruited, trained, remunerated and motivated within the context of the chosen business strategy. This chapter will outline the course of action typically followed in these areas by international banks and discuss the principal problems encountered in implementing a given strategy.

OPERATING SYSTEMS AND THEIR USE

A bank's operating system reflects primarily the volume of business processed and the position on the life cycle discussed earlier. For all but the smallest institutions, computerised data processing has been essential to process the growing volume of treasury, credit and deposit-related transactions. Computerisation for these banks has been a physical necessity as well as the lowest cost means of data processing.

The design and output of a given system, however, tend to evolve as a bank moves along its international life cycle. In its most primitive initial stage, the system is designed to produce accounting and transaction-related data: balance sheet and income statement items for reporting purposes, transaction listings for record-keeping and client billing purposes, and an orientation towards the individual accounting unit – branch, subsidiary or parent bank. In such a system, the bank's chart of accounts tends to determine the nature of data output.

As the bank focuses increasingly on specific client and product groups and as profitability comes to dominate strategic thinking, however, new demands are made on these accounting-based systems. The most obvious is functional profitability information to monitor the relative attractiveness of clients, products and markets individually or by category. At the same time, a growing network of overseas vehicles with individual lending and treasury functions creates the need for global, real time monitoring of risk positions. Liquidity, foreign exchange, interest sensitivity as well as client, counterpart and country risk must be consolidated and aggregated for decison-making purposes. To respond to practical market requirements, such monitoring should ideally take place on a real time basis.

Responses by individual banks to these challenges have taken a variety of forms. Many banks attempt to gather the relevant information on a manual basis, as the cost and time necessary to computerise these more sophisticated requirements can be substantial. Such manual calculations can be sufficient for decision-making purposes in areas such as client or product profitability where the critical variable is likely to be assumptions regarding the allocation of joint costs or revenues. For risk control in the rapidly changing environment of a dealing room or in terms of usage of an overdraft facility, however, they can be totally inadequate.

Banks with multiple operating units and/or a large volume of risk-related transactions, therefore, generally undertake to computerise their global risk positions as well as introduce automated techniques for more effectively evaluating the profitability of individual clients, markets and products. The largest, or global, banks tend to employ their own staff resources to develop a system which is presumably unique to their requirements. Such banks will use their own or outside programmers to develop the software (operating instructions) needed to produce reports and process data. Over time, as priorities change and the international function evolves, substantial financial commitments can be made to improve systems which after several decades often resemble a layer-cake of different hardware and software approaches employed on different occasions.

Smaller institutions without these complex requirements or the financial capacity to support such an investment have turned to a number of package software systems designed to run on standard computer hardware and to meet the basic needs of most banks active in international lending and treasury products. Because of perceived needs which are unique to these institutions, however, many of them have modified these packages at their own expense to suit their particular requirements.

ATTITUDES TOWARDS MANAGEMENT INFORMATION NEEDED FOR PERFORMANCE MEASUREMENT

One of the principal uses of data generated by these systems is to provide management information which is used to allocate resources and measure performance. As a bank moves along its international life cycle, its information requirements evolve accordingly. A survey such as the one carried out in 1978 thus reflects dramatically different approaches to the need to develop information on individual products, markets, clients and operating units.

At the one extreme are a number of large American banks with highly sophisticated, profit-oriented information systems which go as far as measuring the incremental return on capital or assets of each individual loan transaction proposed as well as profitability by client and product. To such institutions, banking is a business like any other whose ultimate objective is to maximise long term profitability for stockholders, and each operating unit, function and significant transaction must be evaluated with this objective in mind. A total of seven such banks in the questionnaire sample, for example, had highly refined formulae which assume a given level of loss reserve and capital allocation to support each domestic and international loan submitted for approval. Unless a minimum return on capital or assets is generated by the revenues produced from the proposed transaction, or the loan officer can justify the transaction on the basis of a strong relationship, the proposal is presumably rejected. Behind such formulae lie detailed calculations of a bank's appropriate level of leverage, dividend payout, desired return on net worth and allocation of capital and loss reserves, not only to the various functions of the bank but also to different categories of assets.

At the other extreme are institutions such as many Japanese and continental European banks for whom incremental profits, however measured, are only one of a number of objectives for their institution. Such goals may include a strong commitment to contributing to the perceived national interest, maintenance of market share, a genuine belief that they are a service institution one of whose major objectives is to assist traditional customers in international dealings, and a concern for fairness to employees, community service and professionalism which could easily conflict with the profit motive.

Quite apart from such fundamental philosophical differences are the practical problems of measuring performance in a complex organisation subject to a variety of exogenous factors beyond management's control. Many international bankers honestly object to profit measurement in an industry whose fortunes are subject to government intervention, monetary policy and interest rate levels, loan demand, level and volatility of foreign exchange activity as well as the elements of civil strife, war and other characteristics of international business. Moreover, in an industry where losses on the loan portfolio and foreign exchange book can threaten the existence of the bank itself, such critics feel that setting income targets which imply a given level of credit or foreign exchange risk could well motivate lending officers and dealers to make commitments regardless of market conditions, simply to fulfil a given profit target.

At the level of the individual institution, a much larger proportion of bankers consider that the necessarily arbitrary classifications of revenues, expenses, loan reserves and capital funds needed for a thorough-going evaluation of the international function effectively negate the value of the results obtained. The fundamental decision to assign revenue and costs to international, as opposed to domestic operations, is to many a totally illogical distinction, in view of their image of the international function as representing one of the many customer services going to make up an overall package which cannot be broken up for analysis.

Of more concern to many managers are the practical problems both of designing a management information system to provide relevant data, and of making the arbitrary allocations of certain overhead costs and capital to the respective banking functions. Honest managers can disagree honestly over such knotty questions as the level of a bank's capital necessary to support a given asset such as interbank loans, the appropriate allocation of loan loss reserves to sovereign risk credits, and the proportion of senior management overhead to be allocated to the international function. In addition, particularly in European and other banks where major domestic branches carry on an active international business quite apart from the central international function, there are real practical problems and costs of actually delineating the related expenses and revenues associated with international business in such branches or operating centres.

Underlying many of these logical arguments, however, are highly subjective views stemming from the personal motives of the individuals involved. An international banker may be unlikely to support detailed performance measurement if it would reveal the relative unprofitability of his own function or department, while there is a natural reluctance on the part of many individuals to commit themselves to a given level of performance as part of a plan target. By the same token, in the case of institutions committed to performance measurement, motives other than an honest search for the statistical truth may be behind such a commitment. In the USA, stockholder and regulatory requirements have obliged banks to calculate and often publish data which the bankers involved would clearly love to remain a state secret. Moreover, for an international function performing well and showing a satisfactory rate of growth compared to its domestic counterpart, it is understandable that the individuals in question should seek to quantify their performance.

One of the major obstacles for a bank making an honest effort to develop useful data on which resource allocation decisions can be made is the joint nature of many of the costs and revenues under consideration. The other side of this coin is the expressed preference by many clients for a wide range of services. As a result, many banks are deterred from making the often arbitrary allocations of cost and revenue which would enable the bank to determine on which clients or products it is making money.

A related problem is that of providing an appropriate incentive to the various individuals and units in the bank to take action which will maximise the bank's overall performance. In a complex matrix-type structure where the involvement of several individuals is necessary to complete a desired transaction, it is all too easy for arguments to occur over which individual or department will obtain credit for the profit element of the transaction. Front end fees on syndicated loans and customer deposits taken at below-market rates are particularly subject to such arguments, which could conceivably result in an otherwise desirable transaction not being completed. One solution to this allocation problem is the use of a totally separate set of management credits or points which are not directly related to the profit earned on a specific relationship or transaction but are tied to agreed overall bank, department or individual goals.

The obstacles to a conscientious use of management information for performance measurement are shown in a 1979 study of 45 US banks carried out by the Center for International Banking Studies (CIBS).[1] Even though US institutions have been more concerned with performance measurement than others, this study indicated considerable controversy and difference of opinion even in the USA with regard to the allocation of many income and expense items between domestic and international activities. Over half of the responding banks, for example, did not allocate cost of funds or loan loss provisions between the domestic and international functions.[2]

For the objective observer, however, the reasonable approach to international bank performance measurement probably lies somewhere between the two extremes. To those objecting to the importance of external variables in determining bank performance, the proper response is to isolate as many key exogenous variables, such as interest and exchange rates, as possible, and establish agreed bank-wide planning assumptions which can be modified, along with plan targets, as appropriate.

To those objecting to the arbitrariness of allocations of capital and loss reserves as well as items of cost and revenue, the proper response is to consider the importance of the international function in many banks in relation to the possible error which may stem from an unreasonable assumption in the allocation process. In banks with billions of dollars equivalent in international loans outstanding, thousands of international employees and dozens of overseas offices, performance measurement *must* make sense. If a given variable such as overhead or capital allocation is perceived to be critical to the decision-making process, it should be isolated and a range of possible outcomes should be assumed to determine the extent to which the actual decision-making process might be influenced.

The actual measurement of profit performance can take a variety of forms. The first is measurement of the profits of a given department or branch, which is a relatively simple exercise in view of the identifiable revenues and costs associated with a function which is effectively an operating unit. More difficult, however, is measuring the profitability of a given product or service which may or may not produce identifiable revenues and often cannot be costed without highly arbitrary allocations of expense. Another difficult area for many banks is analysing the profitability of the funds management or money dealing function so as to isolate the various components of a dealing room's contribution – earnings from matched deposits, mismatched deposits, matched foreign exchange and mismatched foreign exchange positions.

Perhaps most difficult and frustrating of all is the measurement of customer profitability: the bringing together of all world-wide revenues earned from a customer and the expenses associated with these revenues. Few accounting systems are geared for such analysis, which is particularly vital in dealing with centralised multinational corporate customers who have a very precise idea of what they are giving and receiving from each of their banks and do not hesitate to negotiate the best possible deal on the basis of presumed overall benefits from the relationship.

To a great extent, the difference in approach to performance measurement reflects traditional techniques of management. Japanese and continental European institutions have, as pointed out in Chapter 11, historically been run on a collective or consensus basis, and organisational structures and accounting systems have reflected this bias. For such an institution to pinpoint the relative profitability of a given unit or function runs counter to the theme of collective responsibility as well as practical considerations of how actually to produce the relevant numbers. American or British institutions, however, where individual authority and responsibility characterise the management process, are much more receptive to such measurement.

The European viewpoint is reflected in quotations by senior European bankers such as 'The idea of profit centre accounting is not a traditional one at all', and 'I don't think any of us really knows how profitable our customer relationships are.'[3] In addition to these problems of developing relevant management information, banks are also confronted with the problem of a mass of irrelevant information. Banks produce enormous volumes of data – daily balance sheets, long listings of transactions, and so on – but only a small portion is of use to the manager concerned with improving performance. It is standard bureaucratic practice for reports to be ordered by individual managers for their own purposes and for the preparation of these reports to continue well beyond their usefulness or even the retirement date of the individual who originally requested them. From time to time, therefore, major overhauls of the information system are undertaken to improve the quality and usefulness of reports and eliminate those no longer needed.

Responses to the questionnaire indicated a general satisfaction with the adequacy of a bank's management information system, with the qualification in almost all cases that some improvements would be useful. Two-thirds of the 35 banks responding to the question indicated such satisfaction. Those responding in the negative were less concerned about their ability to exercise control in risk sectors such as country limits and dealing positions, than they were about receiving data upon which intelligent management decisions on relative profitability or allocation of resources could be made. For example, all but 3 of 32 responding banks indicated that the basic information in Table 12.1 was received on a regular basis, and those few

TABLE 12.1   Standard Management Information Received by International Bank Management

A. Do you feel you have adequate management information to run your international function?

B. Which of the following do you receive on a regular basis?
—total international profit contribution on a monthly or quarterly basis
—complete description of foreign exchange positions on a daily or weekly basis
—regular deposit mismatch reports showing liquidity as well as profit risk
—complete loan portfolio analysis including country exposure on a weekly or monthly basis
—profit centre analysis on a monthly or quarterly basis showing contribution of major departments and offshore entities
—regular reports on loans considered as bearing a risk of possible loss

exceptions related to the profit contribution of individual operating units. While data other than that listed in Table 12.1 are certainly important in managing an international function, the Table should include the key elements required to manage the essential variables. The typical international bank manager, therefore, is concerned with improving his information flow to eliminate irrelevant reports, obtaining more timely information and receiving it in a form which facilitates decision-making.

Profit determination is a key element of all bank performance measurement systems. In this respect the framework in which profit is viewed is of great significance. In other words, having made the necessary arbitrary allocations of costs and revenues to obtain a 'bottom line' contribution of the international function to the bank as a whole, in what context is the absolute figure placed by senior bank management?

Eighty-five per cent of the sample banks interviewed had, in spite of the arbitrary allocations necessary, established a bottom line international contribution figure in which they have a certain amount of confidence. Such relative agreement, however, does not exist when the same bankers are asked how they or their senior management evaluate the bottom line contribution: in terms of return on capital, return on assets, percentage of total bank profits, or the absolute figure itself.

Of the 35 banks responding to the question, 15, or 43 per cent, consider return on assets as the principal standard of measurement for an international department's contribution. Another 6, or 17 per cent, use some combination of return on assets and return on capital, while an equivalent number take the absolute result itself as the ultimate criterion of performance. Return on capital and percentage of bank profits are each regarded by 4 banks as the applicable standard.

US and Canadian banks tended to show the greatest degree of unanimity in that all but 4 of the 21 responding place primary reliance on either return on assets, return on capital or a combination of the two. Most non-North American banks admit that bank-wide agreement on the appropriate standard of measurement does not exist either because of a lack of concern with profit measurement or the difficulty of reaching agreement on the proper approach. A large proportion of these bankers did not, therefore, feel they could respond to the question. In such a situation, the relative self-interest of the executive involved becomes apparent: the head of a rapidly expanding international function points with pride to his growing absolute earnings or increasing contribution to the total bank, while his superior or domestic equivalent focuses on that contribution in relation to capital or assets utilised by, or imputed to, the international function.

It is the procedure for imputing capital as well as loan loss reserve to the international function which causes the greatest amount of agony in the process of profit measurement and evaluation. While recognising from an intellectual standpoint that the international function uses an often substantial portion of the bank's capital funds, managers find it difficult to agree on exactly how capital and the loan loss reserve should be allocated. In the absence of such agreement, many senior bankers as a second best alternative simply calculate a raw return on international assets figure which does not take income from imputed capital into consideration. In similar vein, many European banks evaluate their own overseas units by entirely different standards: a capitalised subsidiary or affiliate is evaluated in terms of return on actual equity, while a branch's performance is looked at in terms of return on assets. Other banks, as mentioned previously, carefully allocate capital and loss reserves to individual categories of assets, on the basis of presumed levels of risk and global capitalisation factors which assume that the international function of the bank has the same cost of capital as the overall institution.

The relative focus of profit measurement in a given bank evolves as the bank moves along its life cycle. As mentioned earlier, absolute profit contribution or percentage of the total bank's earnings is usually the dominant consideration in the early stages. As the proportion of overall resources increases to, say, 20 per cent or more, there is a much greater incentive to evaluate the function in terms of such asset or capital allocation. Arguments over relative profitability, with both the domestic and international management utilising data which support their respective positions, then tend to be superceded by bank-wide efforts to evaluate the relative profitability of groups of clients, products and markets.

Regardless of the criterion selected or the level of sophistication utilised, most banks have articulated specific profit targets for their international function. These may be expressed in terms of return on assets (say, 1 per cent after tax on assets utilised), return on capital (say, the maintenance of the existing level of return on stockholders' funds) or percentage of group total (say, moving from the present 25 per cent to 35 per cent of total bank profit over a given period of time). The relative importance of criteria may change over a period of time as new constraints appear. For example, the awareness of a shortage of capital may convert a bank from a focus on absolute profit to return on invested funds.

Of all the banks interviewed, the UK and American institutions showed by far the greatest awareness of and sensitivity to the restraint imposed on asset growth by a finite capital base. The sophistication of the US and UK stock markets, coupled with the emphasis placed on capital adequacy by the relevant regulatory authorities, have made American and British bankers acutely aware of the balance sheet limitations imposed by such external factors and the consequent priority to be placed on off-balance sheet income and maximising average loan spreads. Such restraints are much less significant in the case of Japanese and continental European banks which are either government-owned or represent unquestioned pillars of the domestic financial system. In either case, the leverage exercised by regulatory or market forces tends to be diluted, with the result that the use of scarce resources is only one of a number of considerations borne in mind by those with ultimate responsibility for the performance of the banking system.

The 1979 CIBS survey of US banks confirmed the lack of agreement even among these statistically oriented institutions on appropriate performance measurement criteria. Most of the banks analysed treated the international function as an asset investment centre (to be measured on the basis of return on assets) rather than an equity centre (with the focus on return on investment). The criteria of pre-tax income, return on assets, and net interest margins were all considered 'very important' as a performance measurement by three-quarters of the responding banks, while less than a third placed return on equity on the same level of importance.[4]

THE PLANNING PROCESS

The planning process is, of course, an integral phase of any institution's strategic development. Without a thorough analysis of the steps necessary to achieve strategic goals, firm decisions made to develop or allocate scarce resources, and a detailed follow-up process which takes the necessary decisions when goals are not achieved, a bank's strategic plan is little more than a pious expression of good intentions. While it is impossible to quantify the extent to which international banks review profit performance against plan and actually take action in the light of this performance, the available evidence indicates that a relatively small minority of such banks – primarily US institutions – use actual results against plan as a basis of action to achieve strategic objectives.

For many banks, planning and the related issue of performance measurement are little more than a statistical exercise. In such institutions, rough annual targets of asset volume and profit representing, say, 10 per cent growth over the prior year's experience, are set by the chief executive or his planning function simply to show a respectable level of growth. Little follow-up action is taken, and substantial deviations from plan are often explained away by the influence of uncontrollable variables.

The absence of systematic planning in so many international banks can be attributed to a number of factors:

(i) *Relatively low importance of profitability as a strategy driver.* For banks at an early phase of international development, passive service or market positioning are more important incentives than maximising profits. The difficult decisions associated with allocating scarce resources to maximise profitability can thus be avoided. Conversely in banks with excellent growth and profit prospects attributable to natural market strengths, there is less incentive to focus on these decisions.

(ii) *Lack of commitment by top management.* Unless the chief executive and his senior management team are totally committed to the planning process, it is difficult to make the tough decisions and enforce the discipline throughout the organisation over the extended period of time necessary to obtain significant results. The background of many such executives, together with the attitudes described above, is often not appropriate for such a level of commitment.

(iii) *Passivity and fatalism with regard to the ability to effect substantial change.* Many senior bankers believe that the importance of factors beyond their control – loan pricing, regulations, interest rate movements, and so on – coupled with the overriding importance of credit products vitiate efforts to obtain a significant strategic advantage or alter a bank's basic product/client/market mix. They point to such factors as the need to follow clients, the overwhelming importance of interest differential income as opposed to that from higher value products which could be developed, the difficulty of planning for trading activities, and the unpredictability of loan demand.

(iv) *Frequency of organisational change.* Implementing strategic planning requires years of commitment throughout all levels of a bank's organisation, and relatively frequent changes in key positions and organisational structure significantly hamper such a commitment. Banks moving along the international life cycle modify their organisational structure both for good and bad reasons; each reorganisation tends to involve a restructuring of the planning approach with a negative impact on the individuals throughout the bank who must fill out forms, prepare reports and learn new jobs.

On the other hand, a limited number of banks – primarily US – have implemented an integrated planning process with some success and have taken difficult decisions with regard to the closing of units and functions as well as changes in key management personnel. Such banks tend to be those for whom international is a vital (if not dominant) source of profits and for whom domestic alternatives offer limited potential.

HUMAN RESOURCES

In their efforts to develop an adequate base of human resources and to motivate these individuals by an appropriate reward structure, international banks face major challenges. Bankers are as prone as managers in any sector of activity to consider theirs 'a people business', but in practice many international banks have had great difficulty in recruiting, developing, compensating and motivating the human skills essential to implement a strategic plan.

THE PROCESS OF MANAGEMENT DEVELOPMENT

In its relatively passive initial phase, fairly simple skills are required in an international function: an understanding of trade finance procedures and risks, an ability to work successfully with other financial institutions, a generalist knowledge of international conditions, and practical skills in money dealing or foreign exchange. Such individuals are not necessarily those best equipped to deal with sophisticated risks, advise corporate customers on financing alternatives or manage a vast world-wide bureaucracy.

In the American banks which took the lead in the post-war development of the international banking sector, it became evident early on that a variety of measures needed to be taken to develop the necessary management, credit, marketing and other skills. The first logical step was to transfer invididuals with such skills from domestic banking functions with the objective both of improving the skills level internationally and of increasing the level of mutual understanding between the two functions. There were obvious limitations to such transfers, however, as the individuals being sought after were often those most highly prized by their present department head, while the challenge of international banking did not necessarily appeal to all of them.

The next steps taken by many US institutions were the upgrading of their direct recruitment efforts and the willingness to hire staff from other banks. Institutions which had recruited a variety of individual applicants for a bank-wide training programme now began to seek out and hire more high-potential individuals from business and other graduate schools and place them in a training environment which was at least partially geared for international requirements. Banks which had had a traditional aversion to hiring outsiders or individuals from other banks realised that such recruitment efforts were the only practical means of achieving their ambitious international growth targets. Quite naturally, recruitment efforts centred on individuals from banks with more international sophistication. In fact, many smaller banks find that they do not have the resources available to train the staff they need which must, therefore, be brought in from outside. Within individual banks the skills of existing staff were upgraded by the greater use of training programmes in friendly banks abroad, internal courses in subjects such as credit and marketing often taught by outside specialists, and exposure of selected individuals to outside programmes in advanced management and other techniques.

Along with more selective recruitment and training has come a generally higher level of compensation which is also geared to performance. US and other bank salaries have been increased considerably to attract high-performance individuals who might otherwise have been attracted to other financial institutions, while starting salaries paid to new recruits and those hired from outside at competitive rates inevitably caused problems with existing salary structures. Such damage was increased with the hiring of specialists who commanded salaries quite out of tune with commercial banking scales.

While US and a limited number of other institutions have thus made strenuous efforts to develop the skills of their staff at all levels, other banks, particularly in continental Europe, have moved more slowly. In many European countries, the annual intake of new employees is selected without particular regard to level of academic achievement or particular skills, and training programmes are geared to educating such a broad range of individuals in the traditional fundamentals of banking. Only when the individual has succeeded in passing the required bank-wide standard tests may he be considered for an international assignment, from which point on he is expected to climb the ladder of promotion as did his international predecessors for the past few decades. In such countries it is still regarded as undesirable to hire an experienced outsider, and executive mobility has been only a fraction of that in the USA. As their international ambitions increase, however, such banks are finding themselves obliged to recruit a more select group of trainees and to hire experienced outsiders, in view of the limitations on their ability to upgrade existing staff and transfer domestic bankers to the international function.

One of the more interesting developments of recent years has been the reflux of European and other nationals who joined US banks in the 1960s and early 1970s to obtain international training. Many of these individuals have since been recruited back by local banks who are now prepared to offer compensation and responsibility levels once only associated with US banks.

A number of questions were asked in the 40-bank interview sample to determine the extent to which such changes in the personnel development process had taken place and to analyse in this context the background of the leadership of the bank and the head of international. It is interesting to note, for example, that despite the presumption on the part of many observers that US banks promote younger individuals, there was no significant

differentiation in the age at which the present head of international took over his function between, on the one hand,
US/Canadian institutions and, on the other, non-North American banks. The average age of the present head of international
in a North American bank was 45 when he assumed his job, as
opposed to 44 for the other institutions. There would also seem
to be no significant difference in mobility at this particular level;
in roughly 20 per cent of both the US/Canadian and non-North
American samples, the present head of international had been
brought in from outside the bank to head this function.

No significant statistical differential between North American and other banks was revealed by another measurement – the
holding of a university degree by the present head of international. Roughly two-thirds of the individuals in both sub-
samples held such a degree. Finally, some doubt is thrown on the
presumption that American banks have moved abroad more
aggressively because of the influence of a chief executive who
has moved through the international function at some point in
his career. Approximately one-half of the chief executives of the
sample banks had such experience, but the proportion in non-
North American banks was 60 per cent compared to 40 per cent
for the US and Canadian institutions.

One measure of the effort being made to accelerate the
training of high potential staff is the presence or absence of a
training programme within the international function which is
geared towards university graduates. The existence of such a
programme not only brings to light the priority placed on such
individuals but also the recognition that the requirements for
success in an international banking function may differ from
those elsewhere in the bank. Of the 37 banks which responded
to this particular question, approximately one-half had such a
programme, but the proportion of the US/Canadian sample was
60 per cent as opposed to roughly one-third of the other banks.

From the above it would appear difficult to draw many
conclusions about the different behaviour of banks on the basis
of nationality – either in terms of level of interest in international business on the part of the chief executive, the relative youth
of senior management or its level of education. It would appear,
however, that US banks place a greater emphasis on hiring and
accelerating the development of high-potential individuals as
well as being more willing to hire experienced individuals from

other banks. Quite understandably, non-North American banks face greater difficulty in management development, not only because of the problems of overcoming traditional practices, but also because of such very material factors as the need for a banker to be fluent in English, which is the language of international banking, as well as familiar with the Euro-currency banking practices which have been developed from the American model. A particular problem for American and other banks alike is the difficulty in locating individuals, particularly of other nationalities, who are sufficiently mobile to be willing to move from assignment to assignment in a prearranged career path.

A major problem faced by expanding international functions is the trade-off between continuity and variety of experience. In any institution there are advantages of moving both high and low potential individuals from job to job. In international banking, such advantages are obvious: a broader understanding of different cultural and business practices, the opportunity of demonstrating initiative in a new position, minimising the build-up of individual baronies, and the testing in different environments of high potential individuals destined for top management positions.

In more pragmatic terms, an understandable preference for using existing officers rather than new hires to staff positions opening up at home and abroad has resulted in a massive periodic recycling of middle and senior grade officers every few years through a variety of positions throughout a bank's network. The typical young generalist international officer with management potential can thus anticipate a variety of line and staff positions in a number of home office and overseas assignments.

As the degree of specialisation and level of sophistication of international bank products and clients increase, however, the traditional disadvantages of such mobility become more significant. In the days of the generalist banker, know-how in treasury, specialist lending or operations was not essential, and such bankers could move from Paris to Tokyo to São Paulo and still perform effectively.

Local national staff might be frustrated by the reservation of top jobs for an ever-changing new young face from home office, and client relationships would suffer because of frequent changes in account office responsibility, but the business of international banking in the 1960s and early 1970s was largely that of marketing relatively straightforward credit products.

As the level of sophistication and expertise in satisfying client needs and managing the business has increased, however, the trade-off has moved in favour of longer assignments in many positions and the use of highly trained individuals in jobs which previously had been held by generalist bankers. Moving an officer at the level of a vice-president from responsibility for commodity loans in London to private placements in Hong Kong to personnel administration in home office thus has serious disadvantages in the context of the bank's effort to provide high-value services to a sophisticated clientele.

COMPENSATION AND PERFORMANCE

As international banks move along their life cycle, they must increasingly confront the problems of attracting and retaining qualified management and staff. Success in this effort is a function of a number of factors – willingness to recruit outsiders if in-house skills are not available, an organisational structure flexible enough to make good use of specialist skills, and so on – but a fundamental problem faced by almost all international banks is that of compensation and its relationship to performance.

In the early phases of a bank's international life cycle, relatively low and undifferentiated compensation levels could be justified by the generalist, low value-added nature of most job descriptions. A foreign department essentially processing trade-related transactions or building a diversified loan portfolio composed of Euro-credit participations could live with the traditional highly structured commercial bank compensation package which rewards seniority, a reliable track record and success in servicing client needs.

A bank in stage 3 or 4 of the life cycle, however, has become increasingly reliant on entrepreneurial initiative, the ability to conceive and execute a profitable transaction and the providing of a highly specialist function internally or *vis-à-vis* a client.

The most obvious conflicts emerged when banks began to bid for such skills against investment banks and others offering much higher and more performance-related compensation packages – energy specialists, Euro-bond traders, merger and acquisition specialists, and so forth. Concurrently the banks began to compete among themselves for unique talents such as successful foreign exchange dealers, corporate lending officers with an ability to bring in new relationships and experienced bank software specialists.

One result of this bidding for scarce resources, as has already been pointed out, was a general increase in bank salaries in the USA and a few other countries to levels more competitive with non-bank institutions. For many banks the relative increase in international compensation has acted as an effective constraint on international development in view of the problem of comparability with the domestic side of the bank.

Relating compensation to performance, however, is a much more difficult issue given the typical hierarchical bank compensation structure. Individual incentive payments and bank-wide profit-related bonuses exist in most banks, but they are rarely sufficiently substantial or directly tied to individual performance to provide an incentive comparable to that, for example, in an investment or merchant banking package.

The compensation dilemma is often characterised by the question of whether a subordinate should earn more than his superior because of performance, unique skills or other factors. Many banks have set up performance-related bonus payments schemes which permit this to occur in functions such as corporate finance, Euro-bond dealing and F/X trading.

Such incentive payments designed to reward outstanding performance and ensure comparability with outside compensation structures, however, raise major problems of morale in international banks because of the difficulty of establishing what are seen to be equitable standards throughout the bank. The profit contribution of many individuals and departments is difficult to quantify, while in other cases a performance incentive is inappropriate. Latent friction already exists in international banks with high profile merchant banking or corporate finance functions because of the perceived prestige and visibility of the latter. This friction can be compounded by special compensation arrangements. Despite top management's efforts to assure lending officers and others not benefiting from major performance bonuses that all qualified individuals will be given an opportunity to become part of the privileged unit, a 'we and they' atmosphere can easily arise between functions which must collaborate in a matrix-type organisational structure. Another aspect of incentive programmes which affect only selected areas of a bank is the difficulty of paying a substantial performance bonus when the bank as a whole has had a bad year or when a bank-wide austerity programme is applied.

A much broader problem is that of actually measuring performance and relating individual compensation to that performance. In the early stages of international development, little effort was made to quantify individual performance, and salary increases tended to be relatively undifferentiated and tied to inflation rates and overall bank profitability. The advent of a product/client/market approach to strategy implies the need to quantify individual and functional contributions, and many banks have instituted management-by-objective programmes by which each bank officer above a certain grade agrees with his superior on a set of specific, quantifiable personal objectives which are reviewed at the end of the planning period. Every effort is made to set objectives which are both realistic and within the reasonable control of the individual. In practice, however, the play of exogenous variables, coupled with the difficulty of allocating responsibility in a matrix or interdependent structure, have made many bank managements reluctant to use the resulting performance ratings as the primary basis for compensation decisions. As indicated above, many banks find it extremely difficult to determine whether an account officer or the dealing room should obtain credit for customer deposits obtained below market rates, while business development performance can be totally undermined by external factors such as war or a top management decision for various reasons to cut back a lending programme.

As a result of these problems in relating reward to performance, most international banks have found it quite difficult to attract and retain high performance individuals who can obtain competitive salaries and performance bonuses in non-bank institutions. Even when a bank matches or surpasses a non-bank compensation package, retention of corporate finance, trading and other specialists is rendered difficult by the more flexible, horizontal organisational structure inherent in a smaller or more transaction-oriented institution such as a merchant or investment bank.

13 The Performance Record

As in the case of the loan loss experience analysed in Chapter 10, relatively reliable data on the overall profitability of the international function are available only in the case of US banks, which have been obliged by their regulatory authorities to break out international performance statistics. It is, of course, dangerous to extrapolate this experience to that of banks in other countries both because of the difficulty of agreeing on definitions of 'international' and the lack of published data. On the other hand, the leadership role and physical importance of US banks in the international market justify such an analytical focus.

Table 13.1, a summary of the relative growth records of 10 major US banks, illustrates a domestic/international performance pattern which in all probability has validity for a variety of smaller banks in the USA and in other countries.

It demonstrates first the rapid absolute and relative growth of

TABLE 13.1   Earnings Growth of Ten Major US Banks 1972–81 (in percentages)

	Annual Growth Rate		International Earnings as % of Total
	Domestic	International	
1972–7 (compound average)	4.4	22.8	N/A
1977	10.9	8.0	50.8
1978	40.0	13.7	45.5
1979	26.7	9.3	42.3
1980	2.2	19.5	46.0
1981	0.6	8.8	48.0
1977–81 (compound average)	16.2	12.7	46.5

Source: Salomon Brothers.

the international function during the early 1970s: a 22.8 per cent compound annual rate of growth between 1972 and 1977 contrasted to one of 4.4 per cent for domestic earnings. This growth reflected two factors – a deliberate focus on international as a source of incremental profits, and the relatively poor performance of domestic earnings due to recessionary pressures and loan losses.

During the 1977–81 period, however, domestic earnings growth has exceeded that of international by a slight margin – 16.2 per cent vs. 12.7 per cent on a compound annual basis. This result stems from a recovery of domestic earnings as well as a conscious slowing of international penetration as the risk/reward ratio in international lending has deteriorated. On balance for these 10 largest US banks, the average proportion of international earnings has stabilised in the region of 40–50 per cent of the total. Of equal interest is the relative change in year-to-year performance, where favourable growth in international has often (as in 1980/81) countered flat results domestically. Here one sees the balancing or portfolio role played by the international function in offsetting short- or long-term deficiencies in domestic profitability. Bankers throughout the world have cited the relative flexibility and lower cost of the international function in playing this portfolio balancing role.

While one cannot extrapolate on a global basis the cycle of rapid and then slower growth shown in the 1970s by major US banks, it is reasonable to assume that many other international banks have and will continue to experience a similar cycle. Previous chapters have discussed the factors which exercise a negative impact on international growth following the initial dynamic period: increase in the overhead expense of running a growing network, a concern with the risk/reward ratio in credit products, and a greater bankwide focus on products and clients which offer relatively attractive profit prospects regardless of geographic location.

Of the 29 banks in the 1978 interview sample prepared to project a rate of international earnings growth for the medium term, 21 or roughly three-quarters estimated one between 10 and 20 per cent per annum. There was no significant statistical difference between the rate projected by North American banks on the one hand and that of the other half of the sample. Among the positive factors cited by bankers in estimating future growth were the development of new markets and products, as well as the amortisation of the cost of entry into such markets through the opening of branches and the build-up of experienced staff. Negative factors included the current competitive pressure on gross margins, rising cost levels, and the presence of domestic business regarded by senior mangement as offering a more attractive risk/reward profile than overseas lending.

The relative profitability of international vs. domestic banking is an issue of widespread interest, particularly for those banks making conscious resource allocation decisions. US and Canadian banks are the only national groups which provide sufficient data to evaluate this issue, although others from time to time provide some indication of relative profitability. Even for the North American institutions, of course, it must be borne in mind that a variety of arbitrary cost and revenue decisions must be made to provide such a breakdown; not all banks agree on some of the key allocation judgements. Figure 13.1 presents relative profitability data for the largest US international banks for the period 1977–81.

As measured by the net interest margin (interest income less interest expense divided by average total assets), international profitability has tended in recent years to approximate one-half of the domestic equivalent. The need to pay money market-related rates on a much higher proportion of international liabilities accounts for a major portion of this differential; relatively high lending spreads on a domestic retail and middle market corporate loan portfolio is another significant factor. It is interesting to note, however, that the gap is narrowing, probably due to the steady proportionate reduction in relatively inexpensive 'core' deposits in the domestic US market.

Of greater interest is the comparison on a net income basis, which indicates that net domestic profitability is only marginally greater than the international equivalent. Over the five-year period, net international profits averaged 0.45 per cent of international assets as opposed to 0.51 per cent on the domestic side. This relatively narrow differential is clearly attributable to two factors discussed earlier: the lower international loan loss experience and lower level of operating costs for the international wholesale banking function. Should significant sovereign risk losses be incurred in the future, one of these favourable factors will be less significant, while the expansion of overseas operations over time may well reduce the present international operating cost advantage.

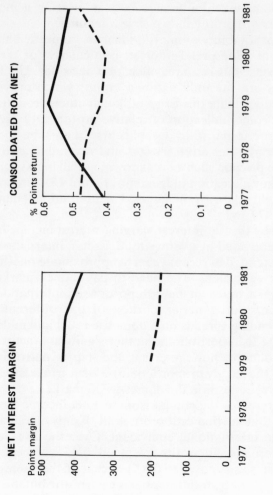

FIGURE 13.1   Relative Profitability of International Banking
for Ten Major US Banks 1977–81

—— Domestic   – ▪ – International

Source: Salomon Bros. Figures are arithmetic averages of all ten banks.

The relatively narrow net international–domestic profit differential in recent years does, however, justify the US banks' efforts to build their international capability. Even if a comparable cost/revenue structure does not exist in other domestic markets, it does appear that international asset growth does not necessarily reduce the overall return on assets and equity by a significant amount.

Canadian banks also publish data providing the breakdown between domestic and international profitability. For the five largest Canadian chartered banks, the average net international return on assets in 1981 was 0.66 per cent against 0.54 per cent on domestic assets; the same differential existed in 1980 as well.[1]

The tentative conclusion that international expansion does not significantly diminish (and may enhance) overall return on assets for North American banks is supported by data comparing the return on assets of various groups of national banks with those of pure international or Euro-banks based in London. These latter banks are primarily active in medium-term interest-differential lending to international borrowers based on deposits taken from the international money markets. Table 13.2 provides such a comparison with banks based in the UK, USA, Canada, Brazil, West Germany, Holland and Switzerland. Pre-tax revenues have been used as the numerator to minimise the distortion of tax rates, the use of tax minimisation practices and various non-operating adjustments to reported data, while assets rather than net worth are taken as the denominator to minimise the wide differentials in gearing between countries.

Table 13.2 shows that pure international banks, or Euro-banks, based in London have reported pre-tax returns on assets which are quite comparable with the overall results of national bank samples throughout the world. Perhaps the best comparison is with banks in countries such as the USA, UK and Canada which tend to use similar accounting and reporting standards as the Euro-banks. During the 1980/81 period, the average pre-tax return on assets for a broadly based sample of London-based Euro-banks was only slightly below those of the sample of major banks in these three countries.

The profitability of pure international banks compares very favourably with that of institutions in countries such as Switzerland, Holland and Germany, although in several of these coun-

TABLE 13.2   Comparative Pre-tax Return on Average Assets of Euro-banks and Selected National Banking Institutions 1978–81

Year ended approx 12/31	Euro-banks (average of 26 selected London-based Euro-banks)	United States (average of 35 major bank holding companies)	Canada (median of 6 major banks)	UK (average of 14 major British banks)	Holland (average of 11 commercial banks)	Switzerland (average of 5 large banks)	Brazil (average of 13 major commercial banks)	Germany (average of 13 major commercial banks)
1978	1.05	1.25	1.22	1.51	0.63	0.60	—	0.71
1979	0.97	1.22	1.17	1.67	0.59	0.61	2.14	0.48
1980	1.09	1.20	1.14	1.38	0.51	0.62	2.27	0.47
1981	1.09	1.14	1.25	1.20	0.42	0.54	4.79	0.62

Source: IBCA Banking Analysis Ltd and Salomon Brothers.

tries, accounting standards are not comparable with 'Anglo Saxon' practice. On the other hand, in high growth, closed national markets such as Brazil, international profitability is clearly well below that experienced by local institutions.

Another interesting comparison is that of trends in profitability in recent years. While the 1978–81 data only imperfectly reflects trends in real banking profits in many of these countries, it is clear from published reports that domestic profits have been under severe pressure in the late 1970s and early 1980s in most major OECD countries. The data in Table 13.2 in all likelihood reflects growing international earnings consciously used to offset such negative domestic experience and prospects. In contrast to deteriorating profitability in countries such as Germany, the UK and Holland, the Euro-bank sample's return on assets remained broadly unchanged during the 1977–81 period.

While any such comparison has only limited value because of national variances in accounting practice, different levels of gearing and other factors, it would appear that a Euro-currency loan portfolio funded primarily from wholesale money market deposits can produce an unexciting but acceptable yield on risk assets compared to domestic lending which may involve wider net interest margins but higher levels of operating and loan loss expense. More favourable loan loss experience internationally, with the exception of the Euro-banks which in the mid-1970s suffered from property or shipping losses, has improved the picture for international lending, while the presence of significant fee and non-credit related earnings in the case of some Euro-banks has produced returns on assets and capital which compare very favourably with domestic results. For those without the ability to exploit higher value-added products and the superior compensation which goes with this capability, however, the results of pure international banks tend to lag behind those of their domestic parents.

One can tentatively conclude on the basis of experience to date that, by and large, the net return on international assets is not significantly different from that experienced in most domestic banking markets open to international competition, in large part because of the offsetting impact of loss experience, the relative cost of deposits and operating expenses. Enormous relative variations in such returns are experienced by different banks as a result of different product/client/market mixes, network infrastructure, loan loss and other factors. One can therefore better understand the motives for international expansion of national banks based in such open markets.

Ultimate success both domestically and overseas would, therefore, seem to be a function of such factors as a bank's ability to identify and exploit market segments with above-average attractiveness, to minimise loan losses through diversification of risk and a conservative lending strategy, to develop relatively cheap sources of deposits and to limit the growth of expenses. In short, the keys to success in international banking are not all that different from those which determine relative domestic profitability. The next chapter evaluates the likelihood of these tentative conclusions remaining valid in the future.

14 Outlook and Issues for the Future

When the first edition of this book was written in 1978, it was reasonably apparent that the remarkable growth and development of the post-Second World War international banking community had reached a phase of maturity reflected in structural overcapacity and an increasingly unacceptable risk/reward ratio in credit as well as other products. An unprecedented number of new entrants, proliferation of overseas networks and the inability to diversify away from traditional lending products closely tied to sovereign risk exposure had led to a borrower's market in which a growing number of banks were concerned about unacceptable risk-adjusted returns on assets and shareholders' funds.

Yet the pious principles about risk and reward expressed after the crises of confidence in 1970 and 1974 were once again overwhelmed by the imperatives of planned profit targets, the perceived need to develop and maintain customer relationships and the understandable human desire to do business even at marginal returns rather than dismantle or mothball the international infrastructure established in the 1960s and 1970s. The banker's dilemma was expressed in statements such as 'Certainly we would have second thoughts about getting into it today. But now that we have the position, it makes sense to stay in'; 'International banking, despite its problems, will continue to be more profitable than European domestic banking'; and 'It's not a way to make money. It's a way to avoid losing business'.[1]

The shocks to bankers' confidence represented by the sovereign loan reschedulings of the early 1980s, however, has brought about a response broadly similar to the 1974 crisis of confidence unleashed by the failure of Bankhaus Herstatt. As in 1970 and 1974, the consequences promise to be proportionate to the leap of faith made in lending practices and the size of potential losses. Virtually any bank's credit exposure involves a leap of faith in the sense of extending credit on the basis of assumptions which cannot be proven but are believed reasonable. The international banks' assumptions that sovereign borrowers would or could manage their affairs so as to service their foreign currency obligations represents such a leap of faith, and the cumulative impact of reschedulings culminating in Mexico's 1982 problems would appear to have undermined the fundamental assumptions underpinning the postwar development of international bank lending. In contrast to 1978, when bankers complained about a borrower's market but continued to pursue traditional lending practices, the outlook in 1982 was dominated by fundamental concern over the viability of a lending-based strategy.

HOW BANKERS PERCEIVE THE FUTURE

The change in perception is perhaps best shown by comparing the 40-bank survey carried out in mid-1978 for the first edition of this book with that prepared in early 1982 by the Group of Thirty.[2]

In the 1978 survey 40 senior bankers were asked to rank what they regarded as the most serious long-term threats to their international business. The greatest preoccupation of the 29 senior bankers responding to the question was competition and its impact on gross margins. This was cited by 10, or one-third, as their single greatest concern for the long term. North American bankers were particularly concerned about competition; roughly half of the 15 US and Canadians as against only 3, or 21 per cent, of the 14 other bankers gave top priority to this preoccupation. Such a split in attitudes was reflected in market trends where Japanese and European banks seemed to be playing a relatively more aggressive role in syndicated credits at the expense of US institutions concerned with the trend in loan pricing.

Somewhat more surprising was the emphasis placed by many banks on human resources ('shortage of trained and capable staff') which was ranked as their primary concern by the next largest number of bankers – 9, or 31 per cent of the total. More non-North American banks (5 out of 14) were thus concerned about people than competition (3) or loan losses (3). Given the somewhat late arrival on the international scene of many such banks and their relative shortage of corporate credit and other international banking skills, such an emphasis on qualified staff is quite understandable.

A distant third on the list of top bankerly worries was loan losses – from developing countries or any other type of customer. Only 3 of the 29 thus gave top priority to such losses; none of these was a North American banker. Most bankers interviewed expressed their firm conviction that the relatively good payments record of sovereign and bank borrowers would continue and that their loan loss performance would remain more favourable than that of their domestic colleagues.

Other potential problems seemed to be of relatively little concern to the bankers interviewed. Five gave high ranking to the problem posed by a world-wide depression or political cataclysm and four were concerned about losses not related to developing countries. While a few voiced concern about another Herstatt-type crisis of confidence, most felt that the system could cope at least as well as it did in 1974 with such a problem. Several bankers were frank to admit that the greatest practical threat to their international business was the relative attractiveness of domestic business in their bank and their resulting inability to do business and therefore retain good people, clients and the infrastructure necessary to re-enter the international market at a future point in time.

From this questionnaire there thus emerges a picture of global concern with the obvious short- and long-term problem of competition but also an almost equal preoccupation with expense levels and the shortage of qualified people. US banks, with their concern for return on assets and awareness of the scarcity of capital, were particularly worried about competition and its impact on lending margins.

European and Japanese banks, however, generally do not share the same concern for scarcity of capital funds and, therefore, were somewhat less agitated by competitive pressures. Their principal preoccupation was shortage of qualified people – credit, marketing staff and senior management – to cope with the aggressive expansion programmes on which they have embarked. While American and Canadian banks were aware of their human resource constraints, a number of the more mature institutions were trying to cope with almost the opposite problem – that of placing returning expatriate officers in home office jobs which they will regard as sufficiently challenging in comparison with their experience abroad.

By early 1982, when the Group of Thirty questioned a broad sample of 111 international banks on their plans and concerns for the future, priorities had clearly changed. On the positive side, about 75 per cent of the respondents expected their international lending and earnings to continue growing faster than the domestic equivalent over the next five years. The same proportion confirmed that international lending in the past five years had been at least as profitable as domestic lending.

On the other hand, over 40 per cent of the banks felt that international lending risks would increase substantially in the next five years. More specifically, the main threat to the banking system was perceived to be the growing amount and number of reschedulings. The most serious threats to individual banks, in order of seriousness, were perceived to be:

- default by a major borrowing country
- large numbers and amounts of reschedulings
- mismatch losses (F/X and deposits).

In the interbank market, about half of the respondents felt that interbank activity had become more risky as a result of the change in composition of participants – specifically towards smaller institutions and those from developing countries.

These and other studies point up the growing conflict between international lending as an activity perceived to be relatively profitable and with good growth potential and one which carries a sharply rising risk level almost regardless of the compensation earned. The balance of this chapter will examine in more detail how international bankers may try to resolve their problems and what unresolved issues may exist for the future.

POSSIBLE FUTURE MANAGEMENT RESPONSES

The seven major environmental challenges faced by international banks were discussed earlier in Chapter 3. Table 14.1 lists in summary form some likely responses to these challenges and possible strategic consequences for the banks of such responses.

(i) *Competition:* competitive pressure on a bank's internation-

ENVIRONMENTAL IMPULSE	MANAGEMENT RESPONSES	STRATEGIC CONSEQUENCES
1. Competition	Diversify	Fee or expertise-based products
2. Corporate Client Needs	Client orientation	New M.I.S. and organisational structure; upgrade staff
3. Technology	New investment	High cost of deposits; new products
4. Money Markets	Centralise; better controls	Vulnerability to loss
5. Sovereign exposure	More analysis; shift to corporate borrowers	Higher losses; systemic vulnerability
6. Operating costs	New investment; evaluate all functions/products	Selectivity; new M.I.S. needs
7. Regulatory	Capital adequacy; markets open up	Focus on R.O.A.; define strategy

TABLE 14.1 Management Responses

al revenue base is likely to be met primarily by diversification away from relatively unsophisticated products prone to price competition from a variety of banks, such as medium-term unsecured syndicated lending to prime borrowers, towards higher value-added, expertise-based products such as non-recourse project lending or multicurrency export incentive-based packages. In non-credit products, banks will provide more sophisticated cash management systems to replace traditional deposit/funds transfer products.

(ii) *Corporate client needs:* banks will increasingly orient their organisational structure and marketing strategy towards the expressed needs of major corporate clients. The requirements for sophisticated products provided in a responsive fashion are obliging banks to upgrade the skills of their calling officers, develop better client-based management information to determine the true profitability of such relationships and restructure organisational frameworks away from a functional or geographic orientation.

(iii) *Technology:* new data processing and communications technology is obliging international banks to invest substantial new funds both to obtain a competitive advantage as well as to remain competitive with their peers. Money transmission or cash management systems will be the principal focus of such investment, which will move money more efficiently but will concurrently increase the fixed cost of a bank's deposit products. New products will emerge from such capital investment, but their incremental profitability may well be uncertain.

(iv) *Money markets:* increased concern over the potential profitability and risks of a global treasury operation will lead to more centralised, integrated management with a focus on controls exercised on a real time, consolidated basis. More integration of overseas dealing networks will be accompanied by a comparable merging of domestic and international treasury functions. Investment in improved management information systems will enable banks to measure and evaluate risk, but substantial vulnerability to loss will remain in view of the need to take an interest or exchange rate view in a highly competitive marketplace.

(v) *Sovereign exposure:* banks have responded to the perception of increased risk in sovereign lending by devoting more resources to sovereign risk analysis and emphasising the priority placed on corporate lending without such a cross-border risk. The wave of reschedulings of the early 1980s, however, will have a severe impact on bank profitability as well as increasing the risk of a severe crisis of confidence in the international banking system. This issue poses the most immediate threat to the continued evolution of postwar international banking and will probably result in substantial changes in growth rates and strategic direction.

(vi) *Operating costs:* the inexorable rise in operating costs will be met by increased investment in labour-saving technology and a thorough evaluation of individual products, functions, client relationships and operating units so as to allocate resources in a more profitable fashion. The focus will be on selectivity and relative competitive advantage. The capital investment needed for improved management information and such labour-saving technology will of course, add to fixed overhead costs and be more likely to slow the increase in the overhead/assets ratio rather than reverse its direction.

(vii) *Regulatory:* the simultaneous pressure by regulatory authorities throughout the world to reduce artificial barriers to competition at the same time as they emphasise the need for improved profits will pose a dilemma for many international banks. In the major open markets of the developed world, traditional competitive advantages will be reduced, and banks will increasingly be obliged to adopt a business strategy which is based on return on assets and stockholder funds.

THE MANAGEMENT CHALLENGE

An observer of the international banking scene in the early 1980s has a much clearer perspective on the nature of international bank expansion as well as some of the flawed assumptions underlying its postwar growth.

First, bank management has relied heavily on generalisations employed by industry leaders which supported this growth but which, upon examination in the light of actual experience, could not justify the magnitude of the expansion which actually took place. The presumed need to follow customers abroad, the desirability of a global network in major financial centres, the assumed ability and willingness of sovereign borrowers to manage their economies so as to service foreign debt, the attractions of multinational clients – all have their grounding in logic and experience, but, when espoused by over a thousand banks from dozens of countries throughout the world, lose much of their relevance and validity. For a limited number of banks lending limited amounts to sovereign borrowers, these strategies made sense; for over a thousand banks lending tens of billions of dollars to individual sovereign entities, they did not. While one could applaud the determination by progressive bankers in the 1960s that banking should be managed as any other business to maximise the long-term return on funds invested, it clearly had its limitations when translated into a lemming-like flood into international expansion.

Secondly, international bank strategy has been too preoccupied with factors over which management has little or no control, such as loan pricing, the movement of interest rates, the loss of core deposits, regulatory policy and sovereign loan risk. All of these and others have a critical impact on bank profitability, but too often bank strategies have implicly been based on such exogenous variables as opposed to those which can actually be controlled or influenced by management action. One senses so often in discussing international bank strategy either a passive attitude by management towards defining an active strategy ('we are all part of the market so why plan') or a sanguine belief in a better world ('spreads have to rise').

In contrast, some international banks have built a strategy based on influencing the limited number of variables over which they do have some control. It is these institutions which are more likely to outperform those who passively follow perceived peer banks or simply permit themselves to be moved by events. Table 14.2 summarises in tabular form six of these critical variables as well as the likely outcome of efforts to deal with them and the unresolved problems that are likely to confront management in the future.

(i) *Organisational structure:* a bank's organisational structure is clearly a variable which can be influenced by management to improve performance. Confronted by the problems of growing complexity and physical size, managements have evolved a number of different structures which attempt to resolve the conflicting goals of centralised risk control and corporate client requirements with flexible, market-related responses and a

CRITICAL VARIABLE	LIKELY OUTCOME	UNRESOLVED PROBLEMS
1. Organisational Structure	Matrix with geographic/customer/market focus	Pressure to simplify; hard to attract skills
2. Product Diversification & Development	Competitive advantage from human skills and systems	How much room? Hard to attract skills
3. Investment in Systems	Many cash management systems; use of plastic	Price competition; high cost of deposits
4. Upgrade Human Resources	Training/recruitment	Higher costs; how to attract key skills
5. Improve Management Information Systems	Better data on risk and profitability	Still need judgement in competitive markets; high costs
6. Delivery System	Network shrinkage	Image problem; hard to evaluate value of unit

TABLE 14.2 The Management Challenge

working environment which encourages and rewards individual initiative and specialist skills. There has been an understandable tendency, particularly among the larger banks, towards a matrix organisation with multiple responsibilities and functional relationships.

The problems of such a structure in identifying responsibilities, responding to market opportunities and attracting highly qualified individuals, however, are leading many banks towards a simpler structure either keyed to a single organisational dimension such as geographic responsibility or one which is heavily decentralised. The search for the correct balance between these conflicting requirements will continue, but it is difficult to foresee banks being more successful in the future than they have been in this respect in the past.

(ii) *Product diversification and development:* to varying degrees international banks will attempt to diversify away from low value-added products to higher value ones or even to non-bank products. Many institutions will take the understandable view that the incremental gain from such efforts will be minimal given the physical importance of traditional products, the relatively small size of the market for such new products, and the risks and costs of entering new markets. On the other hand, a few banks will make a major effort to obtain a competitive advantage from developing or acquiring specialist skills and systems, while others will diversify into non-banking products.

On balance, the net result of such efforts is likely to be a degree of success for a limited number of banks but disappointment for the majority. The market for such higher value-added products as mergers and acquisitions or cash transmission systems is limited, and the costs of market penetration may not be covered by prospective revenues. The human skills required to operate these systems and offer these products will be difficult to attract to the typical large, vertically oriented commercial bank. Success in this regard is more likely to be achieved by relatively small institutions or a limited number of larger banks perceived as leaders by the banking community.

Most bankers recognise that they are unlikely to be able to offer a truly unique product in such a highly competitive market with little product differentiation; their focus is, therefore, on providing generally accepted services with an emphasis on quality or professionalism. For these banks, so-called 'new product development' is the elaboration of services or products which may be new to that particular bank but hardly novel in the marketplace. A few others, however, make a genuine effort to develop and market unique services. On the other hand, a very large number of smaller and medium-sized banks feel they do not have the human and other resources to develop any new specialities and must, therefore, rely on whatever skills they presently have. What is likely to emerge in most cases is a sharpened focus on existing strengths and a development of more traditional banking services rather than totally new products. Basic strategy will continue to be defined largely in terms of existing domestic strengths, both geographic and functional, and the exploitation of these natural advantages.

(iii) *Investment in systems:* investment in systems is clearly an option open to banks which wish to obtain a competitive edge. Opportunities lie in cash management systems with a client interface, automated dealing and documentary credit procedures, the use of plastic card-based payments systems for retail clients, and so forth. As in the case of the new products discussed above, however, the advantages of such investment may be offset by competition, a limited revenue base, and the high fixed and variable costs of such systems. Global cash management systems in particular would seem to be subject to all three of these constraints.

(iv) *Upgrade human resources:* one of the most obvious options open to international bank management is to upgrade the quality of its human resources through intelligent training, recruitment and compensation policies. This is taking place on a wide scale as banks throughout the world follow the American pattern of recruiting trainees with higher academic qualifications and hiring outsiders with skills and experience which cannot be developed internally in the short term. Recruiting and compensation policies in a variety of countries are being sharply revised as bank management increasingly recognises that paying the market price for human resources and obtaining competitive skills are a necessary concomitant of moving along the international life cycle.

Yet there are serious limitations on the ability and willingness of many banks to live with the impact on compensation and decision-making structures of highly qualified individuals able to command substantial performance-related compensation and relative independence of action outside a commercial banking organisation. Faced with the choice between traditional practices and supporting such policies, many banks will revert to the former.

(v) *Improve management information systems:* another logical focus for management is to improve its strategic and tactical decision-making capability by assembling better data on risk exposure and profit potential. The early 1980s have seen a widespread effort to improve accounting-based systems so as to obtain consolidated, up-to-date information in the treasury, credit and other sectors.

No matter how good a bank's management information is, however, the necessary second element in the decision-making process is the judgemental factor predicting movements in interest or exchange rates, the likelihood of a country rescheduling, the impact of future commodity prices on project viability and so forth. With more institutions making more informed judgements on those questions, the risk of being on the wrong side of the decision will increase.

(vi) *Delivery system:* as banks' perceptions of their network or delivery system evolve along the life cycle, a key variable is a restructuring of the network to provide a more cost-effective support for bank strategy. In practice, such a restructuring will involve the closure or shrinkage of units and functions as management evaluates the difficult trade-off between cost, image and ability to execute a strategic mission.

Many banks will question such generalisations as the need to be represented in major financial centres, while those already there will try to cut the cost of such representation without destroying the bank's ability to achieve treasury goals and service multinational clients. In making such critical decisions, subjective factors such as internal bank politics, the impact on a bank's external image, and the long-term attractiveness of the given market will play an important role.

WINNERS AND LOSERS

Given these constraints and unresolved issues, one can envisage a number of possible patterns of behaviour as banks move along their international life cycle in the 1980s.

One pattern will clearly be withdrawal: a conscious diversion of human and financial resources to the domestic market or possibly to non-banking activities. Such a pattern was originally established by US regional banks in the late 1970s, and it will be followed by many others in the 1980s as a result of the undermining of confidence in the quality of sovereign risk lending. Such a withdrawal is a logical decision for a bank consciously allocating resources between domestic and international functions to maximise its risk/reward ratio and achieve reasonable growth. Banks following such a course must evaluate the advantages of 'mothballing' their international capability as opposed to closing it down; problems of morale, the maintenance of customer and bank relationships and cost all play a role in such a decision.

Such a reallocation does pose, however, some extremely difficult choices for banks facing limited profit prospects and highly competitive conditions in their domestic market. For some of these banks, a selective international lending commitment is a more attractive allocation of resources than a total withdrawal to the domestic market. For virtually all international banks, the retention of an international treasury capability for funding purposes will require some international presence in the form of one or more overseas branches.

Whatever action is taken with regard to resource allocation, international banks can make use of the techniques and skills developed in the international arena. Floating rate loan pricing to reduce interest rate risk, the use of negotiable deposit instruments, arbitrage between various funding markets, and project financing techniques developed internationally may have great relevance to a domestic market. Perhaps more important is the application to the domestic market of the strategic lessons learned abroad: the need for specialisation and expertise, the importance of management information, and the focus on competitive strengths. This transfer of knowledge of management practices may well be the most important 'international' contribution to a bank trying to defend itself in its domestic market against foreign and local institutions attacking its traditional clients and markets.

For many international banks shifting focus to their domestic market as the one perceived to offer the greatest relative competitive advantage, there will be a 'back to basics' focus on trade-related products and clients. In many respects this will be a regression to stage one of the life cycle, but in most cases this more limited range of products and clients will involve more aggressive and segmented marketing, a higher value-added product and improved human and systems capabilities.

At the other extreme will be a limited number of the largest banks which will continue to develop as global institutions. These banks are likely to be those with a strong existing overseas network and well-established banking operations in individual local markets. The capital strength necessary to support such a global capability and the relative lack of attractive growth prospects in their own domestic market will also characterise these institutions.

The so-called global banks will use their world-wide reach as a major competititive tool with clients who require a truly global banking capability. Whether they number 20 or 50, such banks will constitute only a small percentage of those carrying on some form of international activity. The global banks will share many characteristics with the large number of other international banks which will fall between the two extremes just described. These latter will also adopt a highly selective, targeted approach to international banking, although the number and breadth of their range of clients, markets and products will be more limited than those of the global banks. Even the latter, however, will not attempt to be all things to all clients; global banks like the others will tend to allocate resources away from client and product categories where they do not enjoy a relative competitive advantage.

In the difficult decade of the 1980s, there will be winners and losers among banks with an international activity regardless of size or location on the spectrum described above. The winners will tend to be those who can successfully implement a strategy based on one or more of four variables:

(i) *Relatively low-cost operations:* banks able to tap relatively inexpensive deposits and/or maintain a low expense/asset ratio;

(ii) *Ability to attract and retain high-performing staff:* the quality of people will continue to differentiate industry leaders from followers, and the winners will be banks, both large and small, who offer the organisational environment and reward structure which attract high quality staff;

(iii) *Sustainable product/market/client advantage in a speciali-*

ty area: despite a highly competitive environment and the limited number of such specialities, some banks will be able to maintain or develop a competitive advantage in one or more areas which will ensure premium performance;

(iv) *Global reach:* a limited number of global banks will obtain a sustainable competitive advantage by virtue of their world-wide capabilities.

The losers, on the other hand, will be those suffering from one or more of the following problems:

(1) inability to control costs or obtain good data on risk and profitability;

(2) willingness to follow blindly those competitors or peers who are perceived as leaders without attempting to establish their own strategy;

(3) attempting to improve profitability by moving up the risk spectrum, whether it be in country risk, foreign exchange dealing or interest rate exposure;

(4) accepting convenient generalisations to justify behaviour without taking an independent view as to the risks and rewards involved; and an

(5) unwillingness to adopt the organisational structure and management process for exceptional skills.

In conclusion, the critical variables for success in international banking are not significantly different from those in domestic banking. Given the confluence of the two during the 1970s and early 1980s, this is hardly a surprising conclusion. In practice, the majority of international banks are likely as in the past to move with the tide of their peer groups and be guided by the management traditions of the past.

International banks will continue to be managed primarily by bankers who have proven themselves in a particular aspect of the banking business. As a result their management approach will reflect some of the weaknesses of bankers as managers described earlier in the book: a relative unfamiliarity with and lack of commitment to marketing and product development; a similar lack of commitment to strategic planning and a relative unwillingness to move people and change structures if performance does not measure up. This is not to say that international banks can or should be run by managers from the automobile or chemical industries, but simply that bank management will continue to be a distinctive phenomenon with its own particular strengths and weaknesses. In the future, therefore, one can anticipate that the herd instinct which has characterised so much international banking behaviour is unlikely to change significantly. New products and banking techniques will certainly be developed, but it is unrealistic to expect a much greater degree of product differentiation among banks, who will continue to rely primarily on traditional relationships, as well as their established services and areas of specialisation, to compete in the market-place.

The events of the early 1980s, however, should provide an added incentive for individual banks to move away from the herd and implement a strategy designed to ensure superior performance.

Appendix A: 40 Banks Composing Interview Sample

Algemene Bank Nederland NV
Bank of America
American Security and Trust Company NA
Australia and New Zealand Banking Group Ltd
Banca Nazionale dell' Agricoltura
Banca Nazionale del Lavoro
Banco Hispano Americano
Banque del'Indochine et de Suez
Banque Nationale de Paris
Banque Worms
Canadian Imperial Bank of Commerce
Citibank NA
Continental Illinois National Bank and Trust Company of
    Chicago
Credito Italiano
Crocker National Bank
Dai-Ichi Kangyo Bank Ltd
Dresdner Bank AG
The Fidelity Bank
First City National Bank of Houston
The First National Bank of Chicago
Girard Trust Bank
Harris Trust and Savings Bank
Hessische Landesbank-Girozentrale
Hong Kong and Shanghai Banking Corporation
Lloyds Bank Ltd
Morgan Guaranty Trust Company of New York
National City Bank (Cleveland)
National Westminster Bank Ltd
The Bank of Nova Scotia
The Philadelphia National Bank
Rainier National Bank

Security Pacific National Bank
Société Générale de Belgique
Swiss Bank Corporation
Texas Commerce Bank NA
The Toronto-Dominion Bank
The Bank of Tokyo Ltd
Union Bank of Switzerland
Union Commerce Bank
United California Bank

Appendix B: Questionnaire Submitted to 40 Banks

1. How would you rank the following objectives of your international banking function in terms of importance?

    (a) net profit contribution to the bank
    (b) service existing customers of the bank
    (c) meet the competition of other banks
    (d) develop new business/customers for your bank
    (e) other objectives

2. Which of the following best describes the organisational structure in your international function:

    A. *Decision-making*

    (i) decentralised decision-making with significant use of regional headquarters and delegation to officers in the field, or
    (ii) centralised structure with home office making the bulk of the credit and other decisions

    B. *Marketing*

    (i) functional/product related approach to customers with emphasis on industry or functional specialisation, or
    (ii) geographic approach with focus on regional expertise.

    C. *Interaction with Domestic Banking Function*

    (i) is there a so-called 'multinational' or 'world corporation' group which has line marketing responsibility for major corporations throughout the world with cross-border operations and, therefore, cuts across the traditional 'domestic vs. international' distinction?

(ii) is there a single head of international banking with no other major responsibilities?

(iii) if so, to whom does he report?

(iv) would it be possible to have a copy of your international organisation chart?

3. The Credit Function

A.   *Decision-making Process*

Would you say that you rely more heavily for credit decisions on:

(i) a credit committee which vets most credit proposals, or

(ii) credit limits to individual bank officers who are able to commit to most loans without reference to a committee.

B.   Which of the following levels of loan loss reserve (as a percent of outstandings) do you feel would be most appropriate *in the future* for your international business:

0.0% to 0.5%
0.5% to 1.0%
1.0% to 1.5%
1.5% or higher

4. Profitability

A.   Do you calculate an estimated profit contribution of your international function to your bank? If so, is it

0–10% of the total
10–20%
20–30%
30–40%
40–50%
50% or more?

B. Do you expect this percentage contribution to increase in the medium term?

C. Does your bank feel there is a policy limit to the percentage which international should represent as a portion of the total?

D. Which of the following profitability criteria do you consider most relevant to your international business?

> return on assets employed
> return on capital (imputed if necessary) utilised
> percentage of overall bank profits
> absolute level of profits
> another criterion?

E. What rate of profit growth do you consider most likely over the medium term for your international business?

5. Competitive Strategy

> How would you rank the following competitive strategies in terms of importance to your international function?
>
> - provide specialist expertise in specific sectors which cannot be surpassed
> - offering unique products and services
> - ability to commit large amounts of financing
> - speed and flexibility of decision-making
> - large, loyal customer base coupled with knowledge of their requirements
> - ability to quote the finest/best terms
> - geographic coverage of the market
> - other factor?

6. Range of Products/Diversification

> Do you regard it as important to offer a range of services going beyond the traditional deposit/lending and trade financing services traditionally provided by international commercial banks?

If so, which of the following do you consider important to your international strategy?

- merchant/investment banking
- leasing, factoring and other bank related services
- non-finance related activities such as consulting, equity investments, etc.

7. Future Outlook

How would you rank the following in terms of seriousness of threat to your international business in the long run?

- credit losses from heavily-borrowed developing countries
- other credit losses
- competition and its impact on gross profits
- rising expense levels
- shortage of trained, competent people
- a world depression or political cataclysm which is effectively beyond the power of individual bankers to prevent
- a crisis of banking confidence such as Herstatt which becomes a self-fulfilling prophecy
- another problem?

8. Staffing:

(a) what was the age of the present head of international when he assumed this job?

(b) how many years had he been with the bank before assuming this function?

(c) did the bank's present chief executive pass through the international function as part of his career path?

(d) does the present head of international have a university degree?

(e) how many employees are there in the international function?

(f) can you estimate the amount of international profits per international employee?

(g) does the international department have its own specific training programme for university graduates?

9. Overseas Network:

A. Which of the following best describes your strategy in establishing an overseas banking network?

- offices/branches which do extensive local as well as international business in a large number of national markets abroad
- offices/branches in most or all of the world's leading financial centres which primarily carry on international business
- offices/branches only in a limited number of offshore centres so as to permit home office access to the international market
- no offshore offices beyond a limited number of representatives who do not do business directly

B. Would you say that your overseas network is

- largely in place (based on present market circumstances)
- a significant expansion still to occur
- at the beginning of a major expansion phase

C. Which of the following best describes your attitude to consortium/joint venture operations?

- would never consider them
- only if it is the only way to penetrate a given market
- very useful and appropriate for your organisation

D. Which of the following best describes your attitude to the profitability of a given offshore entity?

- profits are attributed to each offshore office/implantation and the office is closed/merged with another if a minimum profit contribution is not achieved

- we try to measure the profit contribution of most or all of the entities but would place a high value on non-financial considerations in opening or closing an office
- profitability of individual offices is not of major importance in evaluating individual parts of the network

10. Management Information:

A. Do you feel you have adequate management information to run your international function?

B. Which of the following do you receive on a regular basis?

- total international profit contribution on a monthly or quarterly basis
- complete description of F/X positions on a daily or weekly basis
- regular deposit mismatch reports showing liquidity as well as profit risk
- complete loan portfolio analysis including country exposure on a weekly or monthly basis
- profit centre analysis on a monthly or quarterly basis showing contribution of major departments and offshore entities
- regular reports on loans considered as bearing a risk of possible loss

Appendix C: Questionnaire Submitted to 30 Senior Corporate Financial Officers

1. *Selection of International Banks*

    A. Are there any circumstances under which you would add to the list of banks presently providing international services to you? Do you actually discourage 'cold calls' by banks which have no present relationship with you?

    B. If you are prepared to add to your list of banks, could you list, in order of importance, the criteria on which such a bank would be selected?

    - willingness to assume credit risk (such as country credit) others not prepared to take
    - fineness of their terms (spread, maturity, etc.)
    - personal relationships which facilitate doing business together
    - new or imaginative solution to a problem
    - speed and responsiveness of decision-making process
    - size of the commitment they can make
    - comprehensive range of services
    - another criterion?

2. *Evaluation of Banks' Marketing Approach*

    A. If you were to criticise the efforts by international banks to develop a relationship with your company, which of the following possible criticisms would be the most relevant?

- lack of preparation/understanding of your business
- lack of any specific product/solution to propose
- inability to commit to a specific proposal without time-consuming reference to home office
- inability to meet competitive terms
- another criticism

B. When you suggest a specific set of terms/credit risk to a prospective banker to initiate a relationship and he agrees to go beyond the terms offered by your existing bankers, does this create a positive or negative impression as to the new bank's professionalism?

3. *Evaluation of Present Banking Relationships*

In what order of priority do you rank the following criteria in terms of evaluating the usefulness of an existing international banking relationship?

- understanding of your business as reflected in the flexibility/intelligence of the banker's response to your problems
- fineness of terms (pricing, maturity, security, etc.)
- comprehensive range of services and size of network
- speed and responsiveness of decision-making process
- imagination in suggesting solutions to problems
- ability to meet your financial requirements from its own resources
- another criterion?

4. *General Comments*

Would you care to make any general comments on international banks and bankers which you think would be relevant to their efforts to develop business with your firm?

Notes

NOTES TO CHAPTER 1

1. Steven I. Davis, *The Euro-Bank: its Origins, Management and Outlook*.
2. Among them are F. John Mathis (ed.), *Offshore Lending by US Commercial Banks*, and D. R. Mandich *et al.* (eds), *Foreign Exchange Trading Techniques and Controls*.
3. Refer to two American Bankers Association Studies, *The Future Development of U.S. Banking Organisations Abroad*, and *The Future Development of Foreign Banking Organisations in the U.S.*
4. Refer to Group of Thirty publication, *The Outlook for International Bank Lending*, and Center for International Banking Studies, E. Richard Brownlee and Brent B. Wilson, *International Banking: Entering a New Decade* (Charlottesville, Virginia: University of Virginia Centre for International Banking Studies, 1980).
5. The reader is referred to Geoffrey Bell, *The Euro-Dollar Market and the International Financial System*, and Brian Scott Quinn, *The New Euromarkets* (1975).

NOTES TO CHAPTER 2

1. Raymond de Roover, *The Rise and Decline of the Medici Bank, 1397–1494*.
2. Ibid.
3. Richard Kaeuper, *Bankers to the Crown: The Riccardi of Lucca in the Service of Edward I*, p. 83.
4. Richard Ehrenberg, *Capital and Finance in the Age of the Renaissance* (1928).
5. Kaeuper, *Bankers to the Crown*, p. 249.
6. de Roover, *Medici Bank*, p. 5.
7. Ibid., p. 372.
8. David Joslin, *A Century of Banking in Latin America*: Ch. 13: Bank of London and South America, pp. 234–53.
9. Maurice Collis, *Wayfoong: The Hong Kong and Shanghai Banking Corporation*, p. 33.
10. Ibid., p. 67.
11. Geoffrey Tyson, *100 Years of Banking in Asia and Africa, 1863–1963 (A History of National and Grindlays Bank Limited)*, p. 68.

12. J. A. Henry, *The First Hundred Years of the Standard Bank.*
13. The Mitsui Bank Ltd, *A History of the First Hundred Years.*
14. Fritz Seidenzahl, *1870–1970: 100 Jahre Deutsche Bank.*
15. Société Générale, *Société Générale de Belgique: 1822–1972.*
16. A. J. S. Baster, *The International Banks.*
17. Ralph W. Hidy, *The House of Baring in American Trade and Finance,* p. 419.
18. Marten G. Buist, *At Spes Non Fracta: Hope & Co.: 1770–1817,* p. 27.
19. Leland H. Jenks, *Migration of British Capital to 1875,* p. 282.
20. Rondo Cameron, 'The Crédit Mobilier and the Economic Development of Europe'.
21. Baster, *International Banks.*
22. Ibid., p. 40.
23. Clyde Phelps, *The Foreign Expansion of American Banks.*
24. Ibid., pp. 164–5.
25. Hal B. Lary, *The United States in the World Economy,* p. 118.
26. T. W. Lamont as quoted in Siegfried Stern, *The United States in International Banking.*
27. Siegfried Stern, p. 212.
28. Otto Kahn as quoted in Stern, p. 217.

NOTES TO CHAPTER 3

1. See Professor J. R. S. Revell, *Costs and Margins in Banking: An International Survey.*
2. See article by Steven I. Davis in the *Banker,* 'Where Can Tomorrow's Profits be Earned?'
3. See Ehrenberg, *Capital and Finance,* for discussion of Lyons and Antwerp markets in the sixteenth century.
4. Federal Reserve Board, *Member Banks' Foreign Branches.*
5. Deutsche Bundesbank, *Monthly Reports.*
6. Federal Reserve Board, *Selected Assets and Liabilities of US Offices of Foreign Banks.*
7. Bank of England, *Quarterly Bulletin.*
8. Bank of Japan, *Monthly Bulletin.*
9. Deutsche Bundesbank, *Monthly Reports.*
10. Citicorp, *The Emerging Role of Private Banks in the Developing World,* p. 69.
11. See Chandra Hardy, *Rescheduling Developing Country Debts.*

NOTE TO CHAPTER 4

1. See American Bankers Association studies.

NOTES TO CHAPTER 5

1. See study by Center for International Banking Studies.
2. See Group of Thirty study, *How Bankers See the World Financial Market.*

NOTES TO CHAPTER 7

1. Reiner Gut of Crédit Suisse as quoted in *Institutional Investor* (June 1981).
2. See Greenwich Research Associates, *North American Multinational Banking – 1982.*

NOTE TO CHAPTER 8

1. James Cassin of First National Bank of Chicago as quoted in *Institutional Investor* (June 1981).

NOTE TO CHAPTER 9

1. See Federal Reserve Bank of New York study, 'Evolution and Growth of the United States Foreign Exchange Market'.

NOTES TO CHAPTER 10

1. See Group of Thirty study, *Risks in International Bank Lending.*
2. Ibid., p. 11.
3. Ibid., p. 56.

NOTE TO CHAPTER 11

1. Lloyd Bankson quoted in *Euromoney* (July 1982) p. 130.

NOTES TO CHAPTER 12

1. See study by Center for International Banking Studies.
2. Ibid., p. 3.

3. Respectively Jan Ekman of Svenska Handelsbarken and William Bateman of the Bank of Montreal as quoted in *Institutional Investor* (June 1981).
4. See study by Center for International Banking Studies, p. 17.

NOTE TO CHAPTER 13

1. See IBCA Banking Analysis, 1981 study of Canadian banks.

NOTES TO CHAPTER 14

1. Respectively Charles de Croisset of Crédit Commercial de France, Albert Coppé of Société Générale de Belgique and Peter Leslie of Barclays Bank, as quoted in *Institutional Investor* (June 1981).
2. See Group of Thirty, *How Bankers See the World Financial Market.*

Bibliography

American Bankers Association (studies prepared by Peter Merrill Associates assisted by Steven I. Davis), *The Future Development of US Banking Organisations Abroad*, and *The Future Development of Foreign Banking Organisations in the US* (Washington: January, 1981). ✓

Baker, James C. and Bradford, M. Gerald, *American Banks Abroad: Edge Act Companies and Multinational Banking* (London: Praeger, 1974).

Bank for International Settlements, *Annual Reports*.

Bank of England, *Quarterly Bulletin*.

Bank of Japan, *Monthly Bulletins*.

Baster, A. J. S., *The International Banks* (London: King, 1935).

Bell, Geoffrey, *The Euro-dollar Market and the International Financial System* (London: Macmillan, 1973).

Bennett, Edward W. *Germany and the Diplomacy of the Financial Crisis, 1931* (Cambridge, Mass: Harvard University Press, 1962).

✓Blunden, George, 'The Supervision of the UK Banking System', *Bank of England Quarterly Bulletin*, 15 (1975) 188–94.

Brimmer, Andrew F. 'American International Banking: Recent Trends and Prospects', paper at Banking Conference, April 1976.

Buist, Marten G., *At Spes Non Fracta: Hope and Co., 1770–1817* (The Hague: Nijhoff, 1974).

Cameron, Rondo, 'The Crédit Mobilier and the Economic Development of Europe', *Journal of Political Economy*, 61 (1953) 461–88.

Centre for International Banking Studies, E. Richard Brownlee and Brent B. Wilson, *International Banking: Entering a New Decade* (University of Virginia Center for International Studies, 1980).

Citicorp, *The Emerging Role of Private Banks in the Developing World*, by Dr Irving S. Friedman (New York: 1977).

Collis, Maurice, *Wayfoong: The Hong Kong and Shanghai Banking Corporation* (London: Faber, 1965).

Corti, Egon Caesar, *The Reign of the House of Rothschild* (New York: Cosmopolitan Book Corporation, 1928).

Cummings, Richard 'International Credits: Milestones or Millstones', *Journal of Commercial Bank Lending* (January 1975).

Davis, Steven I., *The Euro-Bank: its Origins, Management and Outlook* (London: Macmillan, 1976).

——, 'How Risky is International Lending?', *Harvard Business Review*, 55 (1977) 135–43.

——, 'Where can tomorrow's profits be earned?', *The Banker* (August 1982).

de Roover, Raymond, *The Rise and Decline of the Medici Bank, 1397–1494* (Cambridge, Mass: Harvard University Press, 1963).

Deutsche Bundesbank, *Monthly Reports*.

208   *The Management of International Banks*

Donaldson, T. H., *International Lending by Commercial Banks* (London: Macmillan, 1979).

Economist, 'A Nightmare of Debt: A Survey of International Banking' (March 1982).

Ehrenberg, Richard, *Capital and Finance in the Age of the Renaissance* (London: Cape, 1928).

Einzig, Paul, *Roll-over Credits: the System of Adaptable Interest Rates* (London: Macmillan, 1973).

Farley, T. M., *The 'Edge Act' and United States International Banking and Finance,* 1962.

Federal Reserve Bank of New York, 'Evolution and Growth of the United States Foreign Exchange Market', *Quarterly Review* (Autumn 1981).

Federal Reserve Board, *Federal Reserve Bulletins* – various press releases and surveys.

Feis, Herbert, *Europe, the World's Banker: 1870–1914* (New Haven: Yale University Press, 1930).

Greenwich Research Associates, *North American Multinational Banking – 1982: Report to Participants* (Greenwich, Conn: 1982).

Group of Thirty, *The Outlook for International Bank Lending* (New York: 1981).

——, *Risks in International Bank Lending* (New York: 1982).

——, *How Bankers see the World Financial Market* (New York: 1982).

Hardy, Chandra, *Rescheduling Developing Country Debts, 1956–1980: Lessons and Recommendations,* Overseas Development Council Working Paper (March 1981).

Henry, J. A., *The First Hundred Years of the Standard Bank* (London: Oxford University Press, 1963).

Hidy, Ralph W., *The House of Baring in American Trade and Finance* (Cambridge, Mass: Harvard University Press, 1949).

IBCA Banking Analysis.

Institutional Investor, 'Is international banking really such a good idea?' (June 1981).

International Bank for Reconstruction and Development, *Borrowing in International Capital Markets,* E.C. 181/752.

——, *Multilateral Debt Renegotiations, 1956–1968,* E.C. 170.

Jenks, Leland H., *Migration of British Capital to 1875* (New York: Knopf, 1927).

Joslin, David, *A Century of Banking in Latin America* (London: Oxford University Press, 1963).

Kaeuper, Richard, *Bankers to the Crown: the Riccardi of Lucca in the Service of Edward I* (Princeton: Princeton University Press, 1973).

Landes, David S., *Bankers and Pashas: International Finance and Economic Imperialism in Egypt* (London, Heinemann, 1958).

Lary, Hal B., *The United States in the World Economy* (US Department of Commerce, 1943).

Lees, Francis A., *International Banking and Finance* (London: Macmillan, 1974).

Llewellyn, David, *Trends in International Banking and Capital Markets,* Data Series.

Mandich, Donald R. *et al.* (eds), *Foreign Exchange Trading Techniques and Controls* (American Bankers Association, 1976).

Mathis, F. John (ed.) *Offshore Lending by US Commercial Banks* (Bankers Association for Foreign Trade/Robert Morris Associates, 1975).

Mitsui Bank, *The Mitsui Bank: a History of the First Hundred Years* (Tokyo: Mitsui Bank, 1976).

Morgan Guaranty Trust Co., *World Financial Markets.*

Phelps, Clyde, *The Foreign Expansion of American Banks* (New York: Ronald Press, 1927).

Quinn, Brian Scott, *The New Euromarkets* (London: Macmillan, 1975).

Reich, Cary, 'America's New Generation of International Bankers', *Institutional Investor,* June 1977, pp. 37–98.

Revell, J. R. S., *Costs and Margins in Banking: An International Survey* (Paris: OECD, 1980).

Robert Morris Associates, *Domestic and International Commercial Loan Charge-offs* (Philadelphia: Robert Morris Associates, 1978).

Ruckdeschel, Fred B., 'Risks in Foreign and Domestic Lending Activities of US Banks', *International Finance Discussion Papers,* no. 66, May 1975.

Salomon Brothers, *Bank Stock Weekly* (New York).

Seidenzahl, Fritz, *1870–1970: 100 Jahre Deutsche Bank* (Frankfurt: Deutsche Bank, 1970).

Société Générale de Belgique, *Société Générale de Belgique: 1822–1972* (Brussels: Société Générale, 1972).

Stern, Siegfried, *The United States in International Banking* (New York: Colombia Press, 1951).

Steuber, Ursel, *International Banking: the Foreign Activities of the Banks of Principal Industrial Countries* (Leiden: Sijthoff, 1976).

Terrell, Henry S., 'Some Current Topics in International Banking', paper presented to American Management Association, April 1975.

Tyson, Geoffrey, *100 Years of Banking in Asia and Africa, 1863–1963 (A History of National and Grindlays Bank Limited)* (London: National and Grindlays, 1963).

von Clemm, Michael, 'The Rise of Consortium Banking', *Harvard Business Review,* 49 (1971) 125–42.

Index